Kung Fu of the Dark Father

Poems

Dane Cervine

Praise for Dane Cervine's Poetry

"The Jeweled Net of Indra"...*What a powerful, beautifully written poem!*
"Enlightenment Is A Bitch" *is one helluva poem. The buddhas tip their hats to you.*
    —Sy Safransky, publisher of *The SUN Magazine*

(What a Father Dreams)...is a rich feast. The lyric quality of this work delighted me.
    —Maude Meehan, author of *As If The World Made Sense*

Dane Cervine often lets a wry humor open the door to a deeper place...his finely-wrought poems are a comfort and a compass.
    —Patrice Vecchione, author of *Step Into Nature*

Dane Cervine's poems are at once disciplined, sturdy, compassionate and wise...there's an inspired playfulness.
    —Robert Sward, author of *New & Selected Poems, 1957-2011*

Dane's work brings to mind Rilke's lines from the Duino Elegies: "All that we can achieve, here, is to recognize ourselves completely in what can be seen on earth."
    —Maggie Paul, author of *Borrowed World*

...poems worthy of a long-term friendship.
    —Len Anderson, author of *Invented by the Night*

On Federico Lorca's Notion of the Duende in Art

The angel is the necessary counter-figure to the demon, and its luminous presence floods many exemplary works of art. It seems worth investigating what happens when the angel, a pure being, falls out of the celestial spheres (or is evicted) and becomes a terrestrial presence, entering our impure human terrain. Rainer Maria Rilke is a primary model here...There are striking likenesses between the rising *duende* and the falling angel when they enter works of art, yet there is also a key difference. Whereas Lorca's figure bursts up from below, from the earth itself, Rilke's figure descends from above—it drops down from a transcendental source.

The *duende* (or the demon) and the angel are vital spirits of creative imagination. They are anomalous figures. They come only when something enormous is at risk, when the self is imperiled and pushes against its limits, when death is possible.

—Edward Hirsch

Kung Fu of the Dark Father

Poems

Dane Cervine

Plain View Press, LLC
www.plainviewpress.net

1101 W 34th Street STE 404
Austin, TX 78705

Copyright © 2016 Dane Cervine All rights reserved under International and Pan-American Copyright Conventions. No part of this book may be reproduced or distributed in any form or by any means, or stored in a data base or retrieval system, without written permission from the author. All rights, including electronic, are reserved by the author and publisher.

ISBN: 978-1-63210-031-3
Library of Congress Control Number: 2016946846

Cover image:
'Man Crouching' by Ginny Nagy, 2006, Oil on canvas, private collection
Copyright © Ginny Nagy 2006. www.ginnynagy.com
All rights reserved, no reproduction of the image is permitted without the express written permission of the artist.

Cover design by Pam Knight

Visit the author's web site at http://www.DaneCervine.typepad.com.

We Find Healing In Existing Reality
Plain View Press is a 40-year-old issue-based literary publishing house. Our books result from artistic collaboration between writers, artists, and editors. Over the years we have become a far-flung community of activists whose energies bring humanitarian enlightenment and hope to individuals and communities grappling with the major issues of our time—peace, justice, the environment, education and gender. This is a humane and highly creative group of people committed to art and social change. The poems, stories, essays, non-fiction explorations of major issues are significant evidence that despite the relentless violence of our time, there is hope and there is art to show the human face of it.

This book is dedicated to my wife,
Linda Kittle

Many thanks to The Emerald Street Writers
for assistance in helping these poems emerge.

Acknowledgments

- *Atlanta Review*: "The Blue Horse" won the 2013 International Poetry Grand Prize
- *Avatar Review*: "Finding My Father's Dream"
- *Caesura*: "A Great Civilization"; "Hemingway's Third Son"
- CATAMARAN *Literary Reader*: "Clay Feet", which was also made into a letter-press broadside by Sam Amico of *Middle Earth Editions* – 50 signed copies
- *Changing Harm to Harmony: Bullies & Bystanders Anthology*: "The Rodeo"
- *China Grove*: "The Achilles Stone"
- *Clockhouse Review* (Goddard College, London): "This Living"
- *Ghost Fishing Eco-Justice Poetry Anthology* (University of Georgia Press): "A Great Civilization"
- *Freshwater*: "Meaning"
- *Gnarled Oak:* "On The Nature of Beauty"
- *Inquiring Mind:* "The Noise in My Brain"
- *Miramar:* "Kung Fu of the Dark Father"; "Prophet Motive"
- *Mobius: the Journal of Social Change:* "Lost in America"
- *Monterey Poetry Review:* "End of the Road Restaurant"; "Complex"
- *Pedestal Magazine:* "Copernicus"
- *Perfume River Review:* "The Dare"; *"Where to put a body that will not go away"*
- *phren-Z:* "Spiritual Pandhandling"; "Pink Roses"; "One Life Worth Living"
- *Porter Gulch Review:* "Comeback"; "Moonbeam at the Destruction Derby"; "Beloved"; "The Glossolalia of Poetry"; "Self Awareness in the New Age"
- *Reckless Writing Anthology* (*Chatterhouse Press*): "My First Days Working at the Psych Hospital"; "Butt Crack at the Poetry Reading"
- *Red Wheelbarrow:* "Monkey Mind"; "Caedere"; "Gunning The Engine"; "Rock 'em Sock 'em Robots"
- *Split Rock Review:* "Sumo in Milan"
- *The Border Crossed Us Anthology* (*Vagabond Press*): "While Listening to Nelson Mandela's Memorial"
- *The SUN Magazine:* "My Father's Lesson"; "Wild Weeds"
- *Turning Wheel:* "As My Life Falls Apart, I See a Sign"
- *Van Gogh's Ear:* "Icarus In A Canoe"

Contents

Acknowledgments 8
Kung Fu of the Dark Father 13

Moonbeam at the Destruction Derby

My Father's Lesson 17
The Blue Horse 18
Moonbeam at the Destruction Derby 19
The Achilles Stone 20
The Church of the Mortal 21
Heresy 22
Naked Rebels 23
The *Glossolalia* of Poetry 24
The Miracle That Doesn't Happen 25
The Violence of Young Boys 26
The Amygdala in Junior High School 27
The Best Fight 28
A Simpler Rapture 29
Gunning the Engine 30
My First Day Working at the Psych Hospital 31
A Long, Strange Trip 32
Lost in America 33
Staying Up All Night in College 34
Amateur Night 35
Real Life 36
The Siren Call of the Normal 38
End of the Road Restaurant 39
Finding My Father's Dream 40
A Cure for Baby Boomer Ennui 41

Clay Feet

Clay Feet	45
Sumo in Milan	46
Cigars	47
Complex	48
Icarus in a Canoe	49
Meaning	51
Hemingway's Third Son	52
Where to Put a Body That Will Not Go Away	53
Copernicus	54
Satisfaction	55
Tigers of Wrath	57
The Dare	58
Curve Ball	59
The Rodeo	61
Rock 'em Sock 'em Robots	62
As My Life Falls Apart, I See a Sign	63
Tristan	64
A Lucky Man	65
Lost in Love	67
Like a Woman	68
On the Nature of Beauty	70
Two As One	71
Inscrutable	72
How I Want to Live	73
One Life Worth Living	74
Winter Sun	75
Four Stitches, a Few Bucks	76
The Congregation of the Blank Page	77
Valentine's Day	78
The Minotaur's Lair	79
A Beat Prayer in Paris	80
Invoking the Duende	81
The Dionysian Well	82
Anima	84

Enlightenments

Enlightenment in a Silly Hat	87
Driving Kwan Yin to See Captain America	89
Chance Encounter	91
The Metaphysics of Parking in San Francisco	93
Pink Roses	95
Paradise	96
The Grail Molecule	98
The Noise in My Brain	100
Beloved	101
The Dreams I Can't Remember	102
As the Indigo Girls Sing	103
Comeback	104
Sacrament	105
Wild Weeds	106
Monkey Mind	107
A Meditator's Confession	108
Butt Crack at the Poetry Reading	109
Universal Complaint	110
A Great Civilization	111
Holding On	113
The Privilege of a Private Life	114
While Listening to Nelson Mandela's Memorial	115
Your Thousand Faces	117
Caedere	118
Marginalia	119
Diaspora	120
Spiritual Panhandling	121
The Prophet Motive	122
The Guru	124
Self-Awareness in the Modern Age	125
The Gift of The Fallen	126
This Living	127
This Buick of a World	128
Neighborhood Walk to Circle Market	129
Special Thanks	131
Endnotes	133
About the Author	135

Kung Fu of the Dark Father

Husking almonds on black industrial tarp
spread across the living room after harvest
from our nine-acre orchard where my father,
a disillusioned junior high school teacher,
played at being a farmer. I wanted him

to be happy, watched as he drove
the broken down tractor,
furrowed the San Joaquin dirt for irrigation
from the canal adjacent. I loved lifting
the large wooden-handled mallet
with the thick black rubber head,
walloping the tough tree-trunks
to rain a shower of almonds down
on the tarps we'd haul into our living room
for this husking.

My father's black moods haunted our home,
but I loved how he loved watching *Kung Fu* on TV
while the whole family tore the velvet shells
from the fallen hard nuts as the Shaolin priest
wandered the dusty West wild with danger,
throwing menacing cowboys to the dirt
with a deft flinch of his shoulder—how
my father related to this orphaned monk
lost in the same California towns surrounding
us—everyone, looking for gold, desperate
to start again.

After the show, my father would sometimes rise
from the sagging black leather couch,
place his hand on my shoulder like
the Shaolin's old blind master from China,
and say *Ah Grasshopper, the supple willow
does not contend against the storm—*

though I wanted him to fight,
grab the outlaw's gun, kill the moods
that haunted him so. Instead,

he'd tousle my hair, shuffle to bed
while I tore the velvet armor from one last almond,
swallowed the dark nut whole.

Moonbeam at the Destruction Derby

Everyone forgets that Icarus also flew...
I believe Icarus was not failing as he fell,
but just coming to the end of his triumph.

—Jack Gilbert

My Father's Lesson

I picture him standing in the church superintendent's office,
the grim man threatening to fire my father from his pastorship
in the small town of Live Oak if he continued to attend
the interdenominational prayer group that *spoke in tongues*.
With two small children and a third on the way,
my father must have had balls
to look that man straight in the eye and tell him to go to hell,
that he'd rather resign than resist his own heart.
So he gathered my pregnant mother, my brother, and me,
put us all in the car, and headed south,
not knowing where to go, with no job, no home,
and only a few dollars in his pocket.
Somewhere along the Pacific Coast Highway he woke
in a cheap motel at 4 AM and heard a small voice say,
Go east, so he obeyed, eventually pulling into the beaten town
of Turlock in the dusty San Joaquin Valley, where he went to see
an old Navy buddy named Carl and said, *I need a job and a house.*
Carl said he'd hook him up with the school superintendent
the next morning, because they were hiring teachers. And my
father walked outside to see Carl's neighbors loading furniture
into a truck and asked, *Is this house for rent?* And the landlady
said, *Why yes it is. These tenants are moving out.* And just like that
I had my first lesson as a young boy that sometimes
all you've got is balls and faith. That a voice will speak to you
in the dark of morning with your one cup of coffee,
your single tank of gas, and say, *Go east*.
And that you follow.

The Blue Horse

My mother wakes me at 3am, hands me a flashlight.
I put on old shoes, a jacket, follow her
to the barn where my father is already
kneeling by the white mare. Her eyes
are wild, her breath filling the cold air
with steam. But her muscled flanks
and immense torso know how to do this:
birth the impossible, life
from almost nothing. One egg,
one sperm, small as a thought,
an instinct, a desire. I had wanted
to see this, said, *Wake me
no matter what.* And here it is,
the new foal, impossibly folded
emerging from the mare in a blue silky sack,
as though brought here from deep under water
or an incomprehensibly distant star.
I stare like a virgin. This
a second birth, my own
vanished into bone memory.
But this horse: a kind of god.
In the dead of night,
I kneel in dirt,
watch his mother lick
the liquid sea from his fur,
nudge him to wobbly knees,
watch him stand.

Moonbeam at the Destruction Derby

Moonbeam Avenue was named for the auto-wrecker
at the highway off-ramp in my hometown
who, perhaps because of his name
was the hero of the destruction derby
every summer at the county fairgrounds.

I'd sit in the stands with popcorn and Coke
watching the beat-up cars, their dents
and bent fenders pounded back into shape
from the prior week's bruising. Crushed
headlights replaced. Watch them circle again,
motors gunning, smoky, aiming
their numbered tank-like machines at each other,
careening backwards at high velocity to
ram their steel-barred trunks into the delicate engines
of opponents. It was
carnage and chaos of a high order—
the odor of battle, of fire and metal—
and we sat entranced, watching one mad hero
in this small, desperate town
amid the cracked marriages, the battered jobs,
smash things repeatedly and survive.
For all of us in this broken world,
how Moonbeam would step from the last car running,
wreathed in a laurel of oil and diesel
and smoke.

The Achilles Stone

We were laughing, my brother and I,
flinging pebbles at each other in the gulley—
high, errant arcs holding little chance
of damage.

Such fierce happiness—
pretending to be warriors in battle
lifting, ecstatic, the still angelic muscle
of my arm as it grasped another small stone
then another. The spherical density winging,
falling from an apex somewhere
in the immense safe sky, till

I glimpsed the rogue geometric tilt
of this one rock downward,
just escaped from my sinless fingers,
and cried out,
Run!

He looked at me, still laughing—
and in that eternity
before the oblong stone found
the soft tuft of my brother's
skull

I knew for the first time
what was at stake in this world.
Loving

even the blood that ran down his face
as we stood staring,
his rock slipping
from thumb and forefinger
with his body to the dirt.

The Church of the Mortal

The bowling alley on Bellevue Ave. was built with the same brick as the church in the dusty town of Atwater, where I grew up and attended both regularly. One offered pizza and soda, the other wine and bread. The church, a wooden altar to confess your sins, the alley a wooden lane with ten battered pins you could never quite topple twelve out of twelve times for the perfect 300 game—its own sin. Like the twelve disciples, there was always one to betray you no matter how many times you lifted that dented round orb with the three holes for thumb and middle fingers, rolled it towards the altar of pins, prayed.

At church, I'd watch the preacher, the deacons, the devout ladies cry and holler and exhort us all towards *entire sanctification*, which is like bowling a faultless game over and over. Oh sure, the spirit would come, holy and with hallelujahs, but you didn't have to look hard to see a smattering of recalcitrant pins still standing askew no matter how much you'd holy-roller.

That summer, I began to doubt flawlessness as I haunted Bellevue Bowl, sipping Cokes at the counter overlooking the twenty-odd lanes while broken ranchers smoked and the poor retailers drank and kids at birthday parties threw their featherweight balls down lanes with guard rails up—still never rolling a perfect game. But then,

in walked David, sure, a good bowler just like his dad, but the talented almost suffer more for being closer to perfection than the rest of us, yet never arriving. Like our preacher. As I sipped my Coke and watched the little "X" marks fill frame after frame of his scorecard, more and more bowling disciples began to gather round the molded plastic seat where he sat,

his steely but relaxed gaze looking a bit like a zealot aiming towards heaven. The radio went silent, cigarette smoke circled, and David lined up one strike after another till the last beaten pin on his final throw wobbled and fell. A perfect game. In a town where nobody was without sin. On a blistering day where, for a moment, we were proud, each and every one of us, to be mortal.

Heresy

My first taste of sweet heresy
came from the mouth of a Methodist minister
at the pulpit under an arching roof,
deep purple carpet beneath the congregation's feet
like heaven's lawn,
as he spoke about the Garden of Eden.

How *the Fall* was meant to be—
that without Eve's desire, Adam's hunger,
there would be no *World*,
only the same pretty dream again and again.
I was shocked to hear the world was not sin.
Such beautiful blasphemy,

my high school brain craning past the somber hymnals,
the musky organ music,
the iron gate of the cross,
toward a more complex Eden.

Watching his heretical lips hypnotize,
ample belly so human
filled with his wife's meatloaf, mashed potatoes,
glasses fogging from the perspiration of his sermon;
I flinched as he said
you'll lose everything
till you stand in new skin
naked to this brave world.

I could almost glimpse the translucent snake of him
whispering the human
in my ear.

Naked Rebels

My junior year in high school English
I desperately needed to be surprised—
which may also be why Kurt,
the star football quarterback,
and Mike, the tough fullback,
dared each other to streak naked out of class
at the sound of the bell. We all gawked
as minute by minute the two studs
shed pieces of clothing—a sock,
a shirt, a belt—while the minutes ticked by
and the befuddled teacher, who'd lost
control of the class by now, sat back
and simply smiled. I think we all wanted

to avoid diagramming another sentence
into its constituent parts—lost together
in this tiny anonymous town in California's
immense central valley. Viewed
this sudden improvisation as the grand
thing we'd all been waiting for:
someone, anyone
standing up butt-naked
in front of everyone as if to say
this is me baby, what ya gonna do about it?

Of course later, they did do something
about it: the two students suspended,
the teacher reprimanded. But on this day,
as the minutes ticked down to seconds
and the two boys sat shivering
in their metal and wood desks with nothing
but underwear on, I caught the teacher's eye,
knew we were more alive
than we'd been all year
cheering the naked rebels out the door
at the stroke of the bell.
Blue-jeans piled on the floor
like pyramids to gods
streaking across sky.

The *Glossolalia* of Poetry

Let it come softly the preacher said,
hand on my back as I knelt at the altar
waiting to speak in tongues. At sixteen,
only desire lurked in my marrow.
A darkling spirit just beneath my clavicle.
A form of possession.
Too young to quench it.
No language to speak it.
My tongue fettered here at the transept
of God's house, this small town altar.
Let it come softly the preacher said again,
and I could feel it, the great language
of life billowing up from the immense cumulous,
syllable upon syllable emerging
from the belly—larynx, throat,
teeth—my father's rage, my mother's
absence, a lineage of eldest sons
dashed against bad genetics and evangelical
fervor. This poetry of failure. It all came softly:
the exquisite, dark, possessed language
of the broken heart.

The Miracle That Doesn't Happen

My grandfather was a minister,
fell in love with a woman in church
other than his beloved wife. The story
says he agonized over this apple
in a dusty town near Bakersfield,
finally moving his pastorate
to another ripe field
in Eden's desert. I wonder
what goes unsaid in this family
story? The Bible holds nothing
back: David lusted for Bathsheba
after seeing her bathing, sent her
husband Uriah to his death in battle.
As punishment, Nathan the prophet
reproves David, cursing one son who dies,
another who rebels then mates with ten
of his father's concubines in the public square,
thrusting David's kingdom into civil war
as divine reproof. Did my grandfather
read this before he looked away?
Did he spend sleepless nights
hoping to kiss and not be cursed?
Or to never want again? Praying
for the miracle of a simple,
untangled heart?

The Violence of Young Boys

I was a good boy. Most boys were
in the small town I grew up in,
but not one of us could escape
the peculiar violence lurking
like a mafia hit-man in our DNA
standing in the alley shadow
between the police department
and the library.

Mostly it was eccentric obsessions:
which comic book character would win a fight,
or lining up hundreds of tiny green army men
arrayed against hordes of gray Germans or red Indians.
Our hands like some meticulous,
slow super-computer repeating scenarios
over and over till dinner. Or dissecting
frogs in biology for the fierce fun of it.

Some boys went further, like mad scientists
pulling the legs off a mantis while
it prayed, or incinerating bugs by magnifying glass,
obsessed with finding whatever truth lay
at the core. Even of your own heart:
facing the bully, meeting his fist
with your eye-socket just to see
what would happen.

Our mothers would roll their eyes,
our sisters look confused,
run the other way,
but we knew without anyone telling us
that Darwin, also once a boy, might be right.
That survival required more than calm,
lurked in violent curiosities,
was somehow at stake in each captured frog,
plastic army, black eye.

The Amygdala in Junior High School

Our first brain—which the biology textbook
described as the almond shaped mass of nuclei
lurking deep under temporal lobe.
Like a first love, always with me, fulcrum
of pleasure and fear. In junior high
I didn't have a clue

this fleshy nut was what jolted me
in the locker room when the jocks
flashed their wet towels at bare skin,
or blonde-haired Cindy with her prematurely
dangerous cleavage sidled up to my desk
carved with curses, phallic shapes, letters,
etched herself inside my knife-scratched heart.

Seventh grade was a surreal slide down the rabbit hole
of brain and body as everything grew larger
or shrank in the unsafe bathrooms where I was
just as likely to stumble upon two boys ogling
a torn Playboy page in mammalian bliss
as to be surrounded pants down on the john
with bullies hanging from the metal stalls.
While the small almond of my animal soul
pulsed. I didn't know

when to flee or face the big asshole
who raced across the soccer field knocking our crowns
with his knuckles; or when the tattooed bully
edged his brick-hard shoulder into me
in the hallway. Or if I'd ever become

the leather-jacketed tough slipping his tongue
down the most beautiful tight-jeaned bombshell
I'd ever seen. Her hands in his back pockets
pulling him into the soft lobe of each breast,
the sweet almond of her heart.

The Best Fight

was the one I was never in.
It was high school, I was a nerd
with wire rim glasses trying to be a hippie.
I loved to play basketball. Passionately.
Too fringe to join the actual team,
I played at home in the driveway
or before school with friends,
and of course, in the small town
asphalt gauntlet of P.E.
where anything could happen under
the cocky, bored eye of the coach
who'd steal a smoke while the blacktop sizzled
with our swagger and curses
and wild shots. Shy boy,
I was oblivious to my hubris
nailing shot after shot
in the afternoon's sweaty rhythm
when suddenly this hard-assed tough
from the other team uncorked his battle-worn fists
on my chest, twisting the knuckles
as they burnt my skinny pectorals,
jolting me backwards toward the helpless
foul line. Too shocked to panic, I kept running
down the court shouting *It's just a game,
it's just a stupid game,* improvising
my retreat in the ball's next bounce,
avoiding the cruel instinct of the pack
to form a circle round anyone who fights,
goad them towards blood. It was genius.
The befuddled thug standing alone at midcourt,
his balled fists helpless in empty air, the boys
pulled back like magnets
towards the more perfect circle
of each orange metal rim.

A Simpler Rapture

After school one day, I told Diane I thought the Rapture
would occur in my lifetime, probably within twenty years.
She considered my millennialist passion a curiosity,
hoping for many years, still, to divine the mysteries
of kissing.

I, though, was in love with Jesus,
his passion in the garden contemplating death,
Let this cup be taken from me. Not knowing
I was too young to be craning my neck
past desire's Gordian Knot towards some final end.
Even if it was rapture. Suddenly, to leave
the body's enigmatic rituals, this waking phallus,
this ear quivering with Led Zeppelin,
my quickening pulse. Diane's tight sweater.
Her eyes looking into mine for a sign of something
more than God.

Gunning the Engine

I remember leaving home,
small town heaven of peach & almond orchards
stretching for miles where as a boy
I'd build small desperate worlds in the dirt
while father irrigated the furrowed rows
weekends after teaching Middle School.
Tiny rivulets from the canal became raging rivers
teeming with imagined villages
warring to be free of the tyranny
of small horizons, of entropy, the knot
of my father's Gordian moods.

I remember high school bleachers
painted perfect blue, the crooked
smile as jocks snapped
sharp corners of white towels at me
in the locker room,
the pearly legs and candied
sweaters of the cheerleaders
I could never touch
while immense B-52 bombers daily
gunned their massive engines
at Castle Air Force base
preparing for battle
on the edge of town.

I remember leaving home as Lucifer,
the prodigal son, might have left—
gripping the errant steering wheel
of that old blue Pinto with the flawed
gas tank just waiting for any accident
to burst into flame. Grinding the gears
with angelic arm turned devil,
aiming for the black asphalt with its broken white
pointing anywhere, anywhere
but Paradise.

My First Day Working at the Psych Hospital

I knew there was something wrong
when I peered through the small seclusion room window
at my friend from high school sticking
his finger up his anus then licking it
while staring at anyone who looked.
As though life was shit and he knew it.
I was only twenty, but suspected the brain
might be a bully menacing the best of us
when the charge nurse said the head psychiatrist
had hung himself in his garage days before.
The world

harrowing in its raw nerviness, like
a bad game show where friends
and bosses are playing for their lives,
and maybe me too, only it's unclear
what's behind Door Number Three,
maybe death, or a refrigerator, or
an all expenses paid trip to Miami
with the girlfriend who later ends up
marrying the prick from high school,
all three of us wondering what the hell
happened to the simplicity of geometry,
skipping gym class to kiss and smoke,
and what the hell to do with the rest
of our lives. After working summers
at the tomato cannery in town, I'd had
enough, took this psych-ward job knowing
there was something wrong with the brain,
how it worked in small towns, how
the world could crush it like a plum
in a fist unless you understood how
the bully worked. Knew I needed to
show some nerve, pick a door, any door,
and walk through it like I owned
the whole god-damn world.

A Long, Strange Trip

—The Grateful Dead

My first summer back from college,
I drove to the Sierras and took LSD.
As the tiny drop of acid began to swirl
in my veins, I was peeing from a boulder
amid bear-clover and Manzanita.
Laughing, I bellowed *Hello!*
It's good to be home! Because here
in the psychedelic body, pine and cedar,
oak, the dusty red clay, squirrel, crow,
wind, all so clearly was unveiled as God's body too,
and I, a cell of her fragrant skin. But of course,

after the first kiss there is still a long way to go
to divine the mysteries of bliss. The body
may speak the same language as psilocybin
and cannabis but fail miserably when it comes
to stamina. Can't keep it up, can't endure
more than one orgasmic epiphany at a time.
May make love to God every time the heart beats,
the lungs expand with nitrogen and oxygen,
the penis and vulva and tongue find new ways
to slide around inside of each other. But
after each rapturous moment, the body,
like a bad lover, turns over too soon and snores,
or ruins the moment with a lot of smoke
and awkwardness. The genius
of growing older is learning to relax
into one's own enigma and thereby become a god of sorts.
As though I'd never left paradise—
even though becoming lost was how I arrived
here, prodigal, but favored.
Yet I was too young back then
to know any of this, standing on that rock
peeing into the divine day, thinking the genii
was chemical rather than stubborn love.

Lost in America

I was driving down the mountain on LSD
after a weekend away from my psychiatric
aide job, the only job that made sense to me
in the small town of Atwater. I'd made
the enlightened choice of heading home
still tripping, was keeping a close eye
on the speedometer and the cop car
creeping up behind like a big
black & white beetle with a red hat.
Panicking, I peered into the rear view mirror
and sure enough the little red hat was flashing,
so I pulled over along the side of the road.

The Sheriff ambled towards my window,
began talking excitedly, though in horror
I realized I wasn't understanding English
very well. But his face looked familiar
to my dilated pupils as I focused on
the hieroglyphic sound his lips made,
heard him thanking me for all the help
I'd given him a few months ago
when he'd cracked up and landed in the psych ward
after the alcohol and pain pills and suicidal
leanings. How he'd pulled me over just to say
Hello. Whether he knew how high I was
I'll never know, but he tipped the brim
of his stiff hat towards me, winked, and
sent me on my way—as I laser-focused
my psychedelic eyes on the broken white lines
of a country where I could no longer tell
the lost from the found.

Staying Up All Night in College

She was perched at the border crossing
between *sanity* and a nameless landscape,
digging in her crumpled cigarette package
for one more smoke as she blinked at me
on the couch. As though staring
at the guard of *ego* with his rifle and flashlight—
the light blinding—calculating whether to fuck him
or kill him or just make a run for it.

But tonight in the dorm, she was neither violent
nor seductive, though her blond hair toyed
with her collarbone. It was the fierce argument
of her conviction—

that she would take her life this night in full sanity,
conscious of past lives. That this was her destiny.
That college held no allure, nor the fey boyfriend,
the fawning parents, not the pending minutes,
nor our exhortations that life is worth every minute.

You could see her, while she smoked,
disarming the guard, grabbing his rifle,
running into the dark. Her metaphysics

shaky, her map, if she had one, tugged by a rogue
magnetic pole. But oh she could talk sane—
no judge would condemn, no doctor seduce
with injections of Haldol or Thorazine.

It was late. She stubbed her last cigarette.
We sat with her till we all crashed,
and I dreamt of rifles and flashlights,
of running blindly towards light.

Amateur Night

Yes, I was a male stripper for one night,
well, three. It started at the Dragon Moon,
a seedy bar down the street from my house
where straight, gay & lesbian could groove
together to Mick Jagger & Michael Jackson.
I was in college, an ex-Jesus Freak,
my girlfriend accommodating my dance fetish
a couple nights a week because she thought
I needed to loosen up a bit. But one evening

I drank beer with a blonde Bengali surfer
who stripped at another club, liked how I moved,
said I should compete in the amateur night contest.
What better way, I thought, to strip
the remnants of my evangelical fear of the body,
escape Saint Paul with his distaste of the flesh.

Jesus, though, was Hebrew—not yet made
ethereal. I imagined him loving his body,
the incarnation of it all. Carpenter's hands
and shoulders, firm hips, the navel floating
above his groin like a gibbous moon—

the same moon I gyrated in the bar's night.
To be a man, seen in this way, was like
a resurrection of something crucified, buried.

So when I slid across the neon Disco stage
like John Travolta in Saturday Night Fever,
slipped out of my jeans and pretended to be
a young messiah—women stuffing dollars
in my embarrassing briefs, my girlfriend
winking and feigning a swoon—I knew
my body had been saved. That I was,
finally, born again.

Real Life

Every year my troupe of young friends
made a pilgrimage to the Renaissance Faire
held in Sonoma, dressed in leather and plume,
laced bodice, fur and boot. Imagining

old Italy, drinking Turkish coffee,
sauntering down a dirt lane watching
a horned *Pan* figure high on LSD perched
in a tree. It was that kind of time,

post Haight-Ashbury but pre-something
that kept tugging us like a petulant mother
past college into real life. The

Enlightenment a lost epoch
we ran backward towards
past the horrors of Viet Nam and two
world wars. When my brother

pulled out his saber at the Faire,
pointed it at me, said *en guard!*
I flexed my college-trained fencing legs
and leapt toward him as though each thrust
& parry might carry us both

into a more chivalrous time. Or mystery:
at the kissing booth when my lips
entwined with those of the pretty young wench
who sighed *that was nice*—and later I confessed
to my girlfriend how I liked it.
We told kissing stories about strangers,
past lives unveiled by the Ouija board.

As the late sun settled burgundy and satin
over the Faire banners, we exited toward the parking lots
back into a life real as any stranger—
waving me into the future of her arms,
to live inside her
one long   slow   languorous
kiss.

The Siren Call of the Normal

After graduate school and the study of psychology,
I trekked to the northeastern corner of California
where obscure Modoc County hosted
the Rainbow Gathering, an itinerant enclave
of wandering hippies who would sweep into a rural area,
set up a tented community for the summer, then move on,
leaving not a shred of trash. I hated my life.

My lover had gone. I'd become a licensed therapist
without a clue as to how the human worked.
What the answers were. The unsure science
of the normal.

So I parked my orange Datsun pickup on the fringe
of the forest, packed in my tent, and went looking
for it all. At a far grove of pine,

I found two naked women adorned with only a few feathers
so I set up camp adjacent. But after a week
of weed, guitars, the immense magic mushroom *Om* circle
on the edge of the plateau overlooking Nevada a mile down;
the outdoor toilets, ten wooden holes in a row,
humans squatting like some better animal version of themselves—
yet still no enlightenment, not even free love—
I grew restless,

finally ventured into town. Just a block or two of old buildings,
but with a quaint café. I sat with the regulars
who marveled at all the rainbow shirts, peacock feathers,
blue crystals. They seemed to secretly want
to be one of us. While I, secretly, began planning
how to be one of them.

End of the Road Restaurant

My father once told me he felt like a six-piston engine
firing on only two. After L.A.'s poverty,
father dead, mother on welfare, he wanted to believe
his evangelical upbringing, but drifted
through a young dalliance with the preacher's mad wife,
into the Navy, Korea, back to the bosom
of the Nazarene Church, finally marrying,
bringing his first child into the world.
What was a man to do, then, but raise a family,
go to seminary, become a minister himself
till they kicked him out for speaking in tongues
in the wrong denomination. Desperately,
then, become a junior high school teacher
in the most desolate town on Highway 99
till he couldn't stand it, left
with his family, took us all to live
in a geodesic dome in the Sierras,
study metaphysics, torture a Japanese garden
from the hillside's dusty clay. There was
little money, my mother still teaching,
his retirement sunk into dreams of building.
So his friend Jack let him cook
at the End of the Road miles from anywhere
frequented by faithful dreamers
and intrepid tourists. My sister
sang jazz, my mother waited tables,
and I, back from college
watched my father sweat at the stove
cooking steak, barbeque chicken,
finding stubborn joy late in life
over grilled onions, rinds of pepper—
the end of one road, another opening
in his eyes like sky.

Finding My Father's Dream

My mother finds pink baby mice nested
in the glove compartment of the rusted Jeep
she drives to get down the hill in winter.
I remind her of father's story: a nest under the hood
catching fire as he started the engine.
He'd just been able to quell the flames
with handfuls of snow. She remembers,
asks if I can do the deed now that he's gone
before they nest again under the hood.

I put on gloves, walk to the old vehicle,
open the compartment. Find tissue and chewed paper,
but no mice—just old vehicle registrations
dating back twenty years, a warped first aid kit,
an owner's manual, pages fused with decay.
A dusty pair of my father's sunglasses.

In the very back, untouched by mice,
are two folded pieces of paper with diagrams
for new hexagons—meditation rooms—
he planned to build on the property.
And a still-sharp pencil. He'd pause
in the shade from cutting lumber,
take the pencil out, sketch his latest design:
six-sides opening onto a small deck
like a lotus blossom.

I replace the pencil, the first aid kit,
take the dusty sunglasses and twin pieces of paper
to my mother as I might have when a boy,
hold them in my hands for her to see: dreams
hidden in paper scraps, indecipherable manuals,
what a son carries from a father,
past decay, past any forgetting.

A Cure for Baby Boomer Ennui

At eighty two, mother again recounts the story of my birth:
stopping for tacos in L.A. before midnight
to stave off contractions so my father
wouldn't be charged another hospital day.
I'd forgotten how poor they were between jobs
after his two stints in the Navy. Then my brother
was born, but mother's parents were blindsided
mere months later crossing the highway,
death tilting the world again. We were packed
into the back seat of the old white Buick
and didn't stop till father pulled into St. Louis
where we spent the summer in a basement
wracked with heat and mildew
while he studied to be a preacher. But
that was hell, so mother says we packed
up even less and landed back in California
unannounced with only a few dollars.

The whole clan was devoutly Nazarene,
but God apparently wasn't saying a word
about what to do. So with a few more bucks
from uncles and aunts we trundled from motel
to tiny one bedrooms till father was given
his first pastorate in a God-forsaken ramshackle town
in the middle of California's dry San Joaquin Valley
where no one else wanted to preach. Raised us
with a new baby sister, then another brother.
My mother recounts all this as though it was
the most normal thing in the world,
to be so afraid that you couldn't afford to worry,
even after losing that poor job, then another.

My parents finally got lucky,
landed teaching jobs and bought their first tract home
next to orchards and an Air Force base.
It wasn't till decades later
with two children in my arms and that baby boomer ennui
that I first understood

my father's shame, my mother's fear
when they had nothing but four kids,
a beaten wallet, broken hearts,
and not a sign in the world
that anyone would save you.

Clay Feet

*Neither a person entirely broken
nor one entirely whole can speak.*

—Jane Hirshfield

*My brain's an old rag anyway,
but I've got a woman and
you'd say she's too god for me.*

—James Tate

Clay Feet

All my gurus are human. The best ones
embarrassingly so. The intellectual Indian
with the alligator shoes, fine white hair

brushed forward in a perfect wave over
his Brahmin bald spot, who fell in love
with a woman he wasn't supposed to,

walked away from the community he
was groomed to lead as the new world Avatar.
Makes me trust him more, that he's not

pretending to be human. That he, in fact, is.
Like the Japanese *roshi* whose relentless sake
could not mask the brilliant moon reflecting

through the haze. Or the Tibetan *lama* who
traded red-gold robes for American business suits
and iced glasses of liquor after braving the Himalayas,

escaping death. And always, the women. Who
wouldn't want to sleep with an enlightened being?
I'm not even talking about the ones with the bevy

of Rolls-Royces and machine guns fortressed in
the Oregon mountains, nor the Indiana-bred wackos
indulging suicide in Guyana, or murder in Hollywood.

I mean the regular enlightened beings. I love that
they care about shoes, bald spots, that like me
they need a drink now and again to bear the weight

of clay feet under a tainted moon.

Sumo in Milan

In Oakland at a therapy conference
the presenter talks about his travels—
Harlem last night, Memphis tomorrow—
trains us about trauma, how slow
chronic stress can be more debilitating
than even crisis; how desperate
you can get in a motel before sleep,
watching reality TV to avoid reality—
relegated to body-building shows
sculpting a six-pack, even eight
defined muscle groups, which
as a psychologist he thought a bit much
even as a defense mechanism.
All he wanted was a toned round mound.

I think about my mid-life Italy trip,
stuck in Milan's industrial section
waiting for a morning flight
looking for something, anything
on the tiny television with four
incomprehensible channels,
settling for the Japanese Sumo
competition I watched mesmerized:
immense mountains of men
in white cotton colliding,
stomping bare feet, glistening bellies
oiled for battle, black ponytails
scything the air like swords.

Sometimes you need
to face something immense
that doesn't speak your language,
wants to dominate you,
kneel on your throat,
see what you're made of.

Cigars

The first one scared me to death.
I wanted so badly not to fail this manly ritual
though I wasn't a tobacco virgin,
my father grinning at me with the lone cigarette
in the crumpled package I'd found in the gutter,
ushering me furtively away from mother's eyes
into the backyard where he lit up, told me
to inhale as big as I could. Then laughed
as I choked and sputtered the devil smoke
out of my lungs. He'd been a minister once,
didn't mind a teaching story. Many years
passed as I heeded the Surgeon General's
black labels on each pack, saw the country
ban smoking from airplanes and restaurants,
remembered my high school librarian so proud
of the filthy charcoaled dead smoker's lung
preserved under glass by her desk. But this cigar,

proffered by my friend's father after we'd painted
his house that summer, was another matter.
He was a Freudian. This was an initiation.
To snip the tip of those dusky leaves rolled
on the thighs of Cuban women, touch flame
to its darkness, rouse the orange ember to full body
like Mafia dons and back-room politicians.
Or this worldly psychiatrist inserting a bit of Havana
between forefinger and thumb, who knew
something about this underworld of the smoky psyche
and the lips of men who sucked life's aroma
from its very darkness.

Complex

Freud had no idea what he was doing,
brushing laboratory-grade cocaine into his nostrils
while incubating psychoanalytic theory.
A scientist begins with flagrant hypotheses,
accumulates dead-ends. Who knew
that treating his friend's morphine addiction
with the white powder through frenetic
all-night talk sessions, would result in disaster.
Still, Freud felt he was destined
for greatness. He'd scour animal magnetism,
Victorian sexology, Romantic vitalism,
the Lamarckian doctrine of heredity,
Charcot's precepts on hysteria
for keys to the mind.
For fifteen years his medicinal euphoria
fueled this visionary inquiry
into the psyche's cavernous Id,
finding all manner of complexes:
libidinal, phallic, Oedipal.
Though he confessed to his fiancée
I would give all my cocaine
for one hour in Wandsbek
with you. He was on a journey
that later could be seen
as inevitable genius.
But along the way,
he was as unsure as you and I:
peering into the dream of mind,
recoiling at its complexity,
staggering to the mute couch
for a nap.

Icarus in a Canoe

—For Meriwether Lewis of the *Lewis & Clark Expedition*

He stared at the empty whisky glass
on the cabin's porch railing,
drifted into drunken clarity.
How he'd dared to be a Columbus,
trek even further into Eden's Garden

of buffalo, elk and antelope, wild turkey feeding on hills and plains
as far as the eye could see, deer and beaver uncountable. And
coming down the river towards his canoe, a blanket of white feathers
three miles long, seventy yards wide. And further, the source:
acres of white pelicans preening in summer molt. Cottonwood,
redwood, condor and grizzly, coyote, the Rockies, finally, the Pacific. Paradise,
danger, everywhere.

But now he could no longer sleep,
though he still spread bear skins
and buffalo robe on the floor.
Melancholy had driven him to wilderness,
then mania galvanizing all resolve
in the face of hunger, storm,
the Blackfeet, Shoshone,
the Sioux. Now,

at Grinder's Inn north of Nashville,
he was near an end, though only thirty-five.
Perhaps he was not made for return,
for settling. Mrs. Grinder heard him
pace that night for hours arguing
with an unseen opponent. Perhaps
Rilke's angel who simply refused
to fight.

In the early morning,
Meriwether loaded two pistols,
shot himself in the head with one,
the bullet only grazing his skull,
the other fired next at his breast,
the ball emerging low on his backbone.

After failed attacks by grizzly, malaria,
the outraged warriors, he could only stagger now
to his end—taking his razor, cutting himself
from head to foot yelling: *I am no coward,*
but I am so strong and it is hard to die.

Shortly after sunrise, Mrs. Grinder found him,
listened as his heart stopped beating.
Like any myth, the fall from rapture
the only human return.

Meaning

Hemingway beat the hung marlins
with his fists, a small victory against
the grand failure of a life. Of course,
it wasn't failure, books pulled from
the sea of his chest like the twelve-foot
behemoths wrangled for hours on thin lines
raked across ocean wave. Then hung

in public view. He'd come down to the docks
at midnight with his drunken fists
to dominate the dead fish again,
like a boxer pummeling ghosts
of beaten opponents. What is it

that must be dragged from the depths
of a man? That dies once landed? That

you beat with raw knuckles even after
the triumph?

Hemingway's Third Son

You can never live up to the old man,
though you bear his name, his wrecked
majesty, his blind dreams. The trail

has led through three wives of your own,
seven children, alcohol, drugs, adultery—
wining and dining the demons. It is

a heroic life, in its way, like every son's

trailing in the wake of the immense myth
that bore you. Till one morning you're
found

in Key Biscayne on a curb, naked except
for a hospital gown, black high heels held
in one hand. You had painted toenails,

and as the police approached, you were
trying to put on a flowered thong. The
operation made you more the woman

you'd felt inside for years. Still,

in five days your heart would give out
at sixty nine while being held in a
woman's detention center as Gloria
Hemingway. But for now,

there is this moment: the sun rising
drunk like you with its brash shining
self.

Where to Put a Body That Will Not Go Away

Saint Augustine, skin luminescent with perfumed oil,
wondered. He stood in the Milan baptistery
naked with his fellow initiates who wished
for proud new bodies, incorruptible
as citizens of heaven—unlike other Romans
savoring their tough muscled torsos
in the public baths nearby. The future of western civilization
hung on this question of the flesh—
to be seduced by it, to master it—
though he knew only
his own failure living content in a body
gorged on roast pig, wine, entwined
in the wings of Eros.

Ambrose, his bishop, hoped to abandon the body,
baptism a moment of rapture
as the soul escaped the dark pagan husk
of thigh muscle, dirty foot, arrogant shoulder.
But Augustine worried no single rite,
not even exorcism, was sufficient to solve
the body's dark enigma. He feared living
too angelic, a spectral soul of light.
Still,

his shameless, unapologetic body was tired now
as he offered it to water. If only

his perfumed skin didn't shine so
from the candle light. If only

he knew how to be faithful
to both light and bone, heaven
and stone.

Copernicus

At seventy, he avoids any brush with derision
by nearing death after the first printing of his book.
Who would believe him anyway?

If the Earth spun on its axis, sped round Helios—
the astounding new center of the Universe—
then a ball tossed into the air would not fall
back into one's hands, but land hundreds of feet away.
Birds in flight might lose the way to their nests.
All humanity suffer dizzy spells from the relentless spinning
of this global carousel. Scorn, excommunication,
perhaps fire awaited such a man. *The world is
as it seems,* they would say—

not as a rogue canon from the Polish cathedral
of Frombork pretends with too much time on
his catholic hands. Still, it seemed inevitable,
the truth of it—worked out in his lonely outpost,
observing the planets with only his naked eye
and mathematics (that other sacred text). Reading,
thinking, calculating, with no other evidence yet
possible. But he knew, as sure as he believed
in God,

that though the world is mystery, it is also knowable.
If only he could tell why the ball still falls back
into his hand, why the birds unerringly return home,
why the dizziness he feels comes only now,
slipping from the body's orbit where
neither telescope nor eye may follow.

Satisfaction

I can't get no...

Reading how Jagger and the boys started pure,
only mattresses on a threadbare carpet,
no furniture, a few shillings fed into the meter
for warmth. The goal was not fame,
but to outflank each other with dares,
like returning from a gig to find
a flatmate astride the stairs stark naked
yelling *Welcome Home!* with shitty
underpants on his head while pissing
down the steps. It was a gas, satisfaction

easily had. The band hatching itself
amid poverty, a Vox amplifier, broken
guitar strings. Every waking hour
listening to Muddy Waters, Howlin' Wolf,
figuring out the Chicago blues, just wanting
to be black motherfuckers. Anyone
straying from the nest to get laid
a traitor. Craving

so simple, so attainable. It was later,
after endless satisfactions that emptiness
came. Hashish, blow jobs in the Bentley
called Blue Lena, the Cocaine & Tequila
Sunrise tour, whole hotel floors trashed.
A pirate empire with lawyers, clowns,
hangers-on. Still,

thirty years clean from the Black Tar,
Keith dangles a lit cigarette from those
rebel lips in the Rolling Stone photograph,
sums his autobiography titled *Life*
by saying he just couldn't imagine
living without the god-damn blues—

and I think, *Oh save me from a perfect life.*
Let my fingernails brown with nicotine,
my eyeballs roll up white from all I've seen,
cock murmur from exhaustion,
heart still tremble at the end
from one big bluesy chord after another
till my body falls, my spirit gyrates away,
satisfied.

Tigers of Wrath

> *The tigers of wrath are wiser than the horses of instruction.*
> —Ancient Proverb

And what of the Siberian tiger in the San Francisco Zoo
who leapt, crawled—leaving scars on the asphalt—
finally thrusting her magnificent haunches
over the lip, then beyond the fence.
In one final leap, facing the terrified
young man who moments before had been
thoughtlessly provoking such regal desire.
Was the tiger in her beautiful being truer
than the careless cur who, lacking
the rituals of older men schooled
in desire's wrath, should have known
not to provoke, cavalierly, such raging
gorgeous hunger. And after the boy,
jugular slashed, lay silent on the cold
concrete, what did you, his two friends,
then imagine as you fled, veins
soaked in vodka and cannabis,
Tatiana in pursuit. That your
careless lives were coming
to an end? That some brutal,
unfathomable desire
had leapt, impossibly,
over civilization's
thin fence
to ravage
you?
How
then will you live
after the marksmen
shattered the tiger's skull
as she clawed your shoulders,
arms, your drunken heads?

The Dare

The correct word, he says, is *death*
that had happened to him. Perhaps
it had only been near, but his heart
had stopped, everything just stopped
on a dime. Lucky
to have been in a hospital already
where angels in white lab coats
and fabulous machines pulled his
twenty-one grams of weighted soul
back into his comatose body,
waking three days later to a world
fundamentally changed, though
he could not immediately say how.
No memory of the past month,
including the World Cup soccer match
he'd watched with his sons *(who won?*
was one of his first questions after
the coma). But no matter, here
was life, still, again—and the basic
questions could no longer be assumed.
What to have for breakfast. Whether
to move to India, minister to those
nearer death than he. Anything
possible now in a fundamental way:
breathing, swimming against the tide
of world politics, standing now
under this very sun in the parking lot
of Home Depot where immigrants
still linger awaiting work. Telling
this story. *Each hour*, he says, *a luxury.*
The problem being how to honor the passing minutes,
as though a king had staid your execution,
given you the keys to his kingdom,
dared you to be great.

Curve Ball

His blue baseball cap hangs from the hospital wall,
brain tumor the size of a hardball
suddenly blinding him as though he'd been hit
by a wild curve. In the cavity of skull
lie ghost memories he now tries to grasp
—who he is, why he is here—
questions I also ask myself in the pauses
between innings.

I imagine him in the dug-out of his mind wondering:
if I am not my memories, if I am not my eyesight,
if the part of me that resided in the infield
of this grey matter is gone, then who am I?

He squeezes the soft rubber ball given him by the nurse.
Like a pitcher deciding on a splitter or a slider,
or an umpire of soul picking up the fouled ball,
fingering it carefully, deciding whether
it's still good enough to throw back into the game.

Peering at me with blind eyes,
neither of us knows whether his next swing of mind
will land fair, fall scuffed in the dirt,
or finally lift over the bleachers
as he rounds the bases,
sliding home in a cloud of dust
and elbows and knees.

Like Lightning

At the indoor trampoline park,
a handful of girls and boys cavort
with my thirteen-year-old son at his birthday party.
Their bodies gleam with sweat
in the immense yellow trampoline pit
as they bounce off padded walls,
leap and twist, shimmy shoulders
to the beat blasting from overhead speakers,
hormones not yet ravaging them
but ready, in their shy eyes, arching backs.
Girls harbor newborn breasts
beneath halter-tops, giggle and whisper
as huge black fans cool their flushed cheeks.
The boys ease in and out of the fray,
retreat to acrobatics on the fringe,
then slip into the circle of cackling girls.
It is life, there is no other way to say it,
crouched in their bodies like wildness ready to spring
into blood and semen, elongating bone,
shimmering hair. I remember clamoring
to stay whole as my body morphed from month to year,
taller, stronger, more urgent, brain neurons arching,
pruning, becoming the shimmering highways
the self runs along like lightning, like catastrophe,
like genius.

The Rodeo

The Mariposa County Fair is a small affair
tucked into the Sierra Nevada mountains
where my mother lives. This year I take
my young son with his grandma in hand
to gallivant along the crowded paths
past lemonade and popcorn,
ribboned whirly-gigs, festooned baseball caps,
towards the wooden stands of the rodeo.
Metal loudspeakers hung from the rafters
ask us to stand for the pledge of allegiance
as ragged old men with cowboy hats
and cherub-faced little boys with pointy boots
all rise for the blond high school girl singing
as though the Iraq war depends on every note.
After a robust blessing for all the young men
still defending our country in the desert
where the Bible was born,
we settle again on wooden benches
and begin to cheer for the brave cowboys
shot with a *Hiyaah!* from their chutes
toward the defenseless calves running
wild-eyed toward non-existing cover.

My son sits quiet, till one rambunctious calf
manages to evade the lasso as the horn sounds.
The dusty cowboy curses his failure,
a hundred men sink to their seats—
and my son, enthralled, hops up and down
clapping for the four-legged rebel
snorting his way past the flailing clown
back to his own kind.

Rock 'em Sock 'em Robots

My teenage son brings his garage sale secret
into the kitchen, sets it on the table
next to his Greek mythology homework
about Oedipus and his father. I stare unbelieving

at the vintage yellow plastic boxing ring
with one blue, one red robot, immense fists
catapulted toward gargantuan jaws by the levers
my son and I now hammer, roaring with laughter
as we try to knock each other's blocks off.

He knows the family story, how his Uncle Steven
and I would pummel each other
when the prized Christmas present
first hit the market. Young boys'
aggression melted into play. Some stories

are too dark for play: a father's depression,
a boy's reprisal. How Steven, incensed
at a bitter word or father's sheer absence
grabbed his prized robots and stormed
to the trash pile in the yard,
pulverized them with a baseball bat.

We can laugh about it now—
it becomes a teaching story, as my son
enters manhood's ring, eyes his uncle,
his father. Aims for the jaw.

As My Life Falls Apart, I See a Sign

Driving through Los Banos on the busy highway,
I see a man in sunglasses smoking calmly
in the middle of the road waiting for a gap in traffic
so he can finish crossing. His face stubbled,
sleeves rolled high on his biceps against the heat.
He is in no hurry, taking one drag then another
from his cigarette, letting the smoke drift
haloed about his head, a rogue angel,
the entire scene swirling round the fulcrum
of his implacable patience:

the exhaust fumes, road rage, the endless
phalanx of cars and big rigs going nowhere.
No less expected, no more. My blue-collar
Buddha, my dollar-store guru, a man
dead center in the middle of it all,
unflinching, ash falling on each
pointed-toe boot.

Tristan

Driving toward Sacramento
I pass an immense burgundy 18-wheeler with the name
    Tristan
emblazoned in gold across the back of the diesel rig
pulling two cargo beds of heavy stone.
Of course, the Celtic story comes back to me,
Tristan sent to Ireland to fetch a queen, *Iseult*
for his English king, the mayhem
that follows their love affair spawned
from an ill-fated sip of the magical liqueur
meant for the king's wedding night.
They lose everything, and both kingdoms falter
while the two lovers survive in the forest
on seeds and bark, content to stare
into the drowning pools of each other's eyes.
Though finally Tristan relents, brings Iseult to King Mark,
escapes into the countryside where he finds
love in the beauty of a tangible woman—
Iseult of the White Hands. Her steady fingers
helping him place the rocks from the garden
into the perfect niche of the stone wall
encircling home. Sometimes

love is a labyrinthine enigma,
and if you're lucky, you find your way
on a highway to Sacramento
following Tristan,
his burgundy heart,
his cargo of stone.

A Lucky Man

A wife is a lucky thing,
my college professor said
after describing his fated love affair
with a brilliant Israeli woman.
He was charismatic, a lawyer
and secret mystic, teaching
Religious Consciousness & the Environment
in our small senior seminar.
He told me this sitting in the dirt,
naked, outside the sweat lodge
our class had built in the Santa Cruz hills
for our final experiential exam.
But the heat

had gotten to him, unleashing
memories of relatives gassed
and burned in the Holocaust
ovens. And in this grief

came the other—his love
who'd left him to live in the
Promised Land. The only

woman he'd ever marry
because in their heat
grief and love became one.

Even though she was promised
to another country, even
though vows could never
be exchanged, still

he felt lucky to almost
have married such a wife.
I knew then I wanted

more luck than his:
a real shoulder, each night
to sleep entwined, waking
in love's tangible country.

Lost in Love

> *Teach your children well, their father's hell*
> *did slowly go by...*
> —Crosby, Still & Nash

We saunter across the street, my wife and I,
towards the school to see our son
in a play about love and its vicissitudes.
As we cross the white line on black asphalt
a woman drives by in a Hummer,
yells, *hope you don't teach your kids*
to fuckin' jaywalk like that and
we look at each other dumbfounded.
Who would bother to yell at parents
on their way to see a son perform
in a play, about love no less.
But then, ah, always the cosmic joke
if you get the punch line—how
we almost lost our marriage,
how I wandered, crossed a line,
how my wife lost me years before.
We deserve to be harangued, jaywalking
our way back towards love nonetheless.
How do you *teach your children well*,
the world a cruel stage? But tonight
the failed Broadway play *Almost Maine*,
picked up by thousands of high schools
for its quirky one acts about love,
assures me that my son already knows.
There is the woman holding her broken heart
of a hundred pieces in a bag. The man
who finally learns to feel again
after getting hit repeatedly in the head
with an ironing board. Two men commiserating
over who just had the worst date possible
before finally realizing they are in love with each other.
And the couple still lost in love, fighting over
who was lonely first, disappointed the worst.

Like a Woman

I hate worrying like a woman, I joke to my wife
as we watch the comedian illustrating the female mind
with a mannequin head, wires crisscrossed like hair
all lit up—each anxiety connected to every other,
her mind aglow & entangled like a New York cityscape
at night. She laughs

as the same comedian describes the male brain:
calm and clunky as a warehouse engineer
stacking brown cardboard boxes—each
with one anxiety, one fixable issue—
side by side on meticulous shelves
that never touch, never incite rebellion
in the neuronal streets of the brain.
The condition

that drives women crazy, this totalitarian state
of the male garage mind. This storage system

had worked for me, for years, like the shiny U-Store-It
company with its gleaming orange and silver
metal roll-up doors and the master padlock
with its impressive key. Inside,

it could be messy as hell: your uncle's old
Playboy magazines, rusted toolboxes
with broken hammers, jammed wrenches,
tax receipts spilling from torn paper bags
documenting the thin years and fat.
All of it, if not organized, at least
hidden away. But tonight,

all the shelves are broken, and I tell her
only a wife trained in the art of anxiety
can help me—her eyes firing
like great turbine engines capable of carrying
the whole damned mess of me—
her fingers turning the key in the lock,
her voice purring, husky,
bring it on Babe, bring it…
worry like a woman.

On the Nature of Beauty

Linda and I by the woodpile
entranced by a beautiful dragonfly—
green head and speckled body
caught in a spider web,
wings wrapped in sticky silver,
dangling in air from the shed roof.

As we begin to unwrap the dead jewel
it springs suddenly to life,
one wing freed, fluttering madly,
the other still ensnared.

As the dragonfly in a single movement
twists and is free, our cat Sara,
lurking nearby in the purple sage,
leaps an impossible distance

and inches from our startled faces
catches the dragonfly in her teeth,
runs into the yard as though
she were the most beautiful god
in the world.

Two As One

Sometimes it is not enough to simply love, sweetheart,
so we could turn up the heat a notch
like the article in *Psychology Today*,
the famous yoga couple who build a Mongolian yurt
just north of the Mexican border,
enter a three year, three month, three day
silent retreat—just the two of them—
calling each other reincarnated Hindu gods,
causing their mentor, the Dalai Lama,
to drop his tea cup and issue a warning.

My, my, the heart is wild, and I remember
my own lovers—goddesses all—
how I'd anoint them in fresh projections
even Freud or Jung would blanche at.
So embarrassingly human—
Id and Archetype mixing to make you
one day angel, the next demon.

Sometimes it is not enough
that I am I, that you are you—
like the poor yoga couple, who,
pissed at being cooped up in the yurt all year,
fight with a ritual samurai sword:
she pricks his belly while driving home her point,
then aghast says *Why didn't you stop me?*
To which he replies, *but I totally trusted you!*

Then desperately, how they crawl together
into a desert cave nearby
to further root out all separateness—
to become one. Eventually, their friends
have to send in the helicopters—
find dirty sleeping bags, a bucket of brown water
filled with leaves, each lover delirious, near death.

It is not enough, sweetheart, to love like gods.
Instead, let us kiss each imperfection dear,
whisper what only the human can hear.

Inscrutable

Gabriel, my son, brings a pot of boiling water
up the stairs to my bath, pours it in
because after his bath and my wife's shower
the water is lukewarm at best. He does this
with a little smile, a hint of grace, no complaint.
Whether it is because of guilt, or humor, or love,
I cannot tell. Adolescence is inscrutable, and
he is a master of understatement. After
the third pot of steaming liquid, I say thanks
and he says *have a good bath* as though this
was the most normal thing for a son to do
for his father. Maybe

it is because we both know how fragile
such moments are, after the darkness
that almost broke our family, or
a few blocks away one father dying
from a brain tumor, another already
passing a few weeks ago. The days

are inscrutable. So I let the intense heat
of the bath ease the muscled soreness
from the basketball game we played
at his high school gym with a crew
of other boys and a few gray-haired dads.
He'd made several three-pointers from beyond
the arc, I'd swooped into the key like the old days
with a baby hook: *swish*. A bit of old magic,
a bit of new. Two men, a ball, a bath.
The surprise of it all. The surprise.

How I Want to Live

In Rome, the old poets shouted *Carpe Diem*
when their aging legs began to shrivel,
muscle and quill revolt,
the winter sun dim. To seize

what remained of the day,
savor the last of the red red
wine.

I think of this skiing down Badger Pass
against Yosemite's stormy sky,
legs seizing-up at the end
of the proud long day.
Hot chocolate after

with my eighty-two year old mother
who came to watch, and sixteen year-old son
lounging young and tired after:
Carpe Diem.

That evening round the fire,
I read Japanese poetry
by Ono no Kamachi,
a beauty of the Japanese court
who wrote fierce *tankas* about spring petals
falling as the body ages through
the long rains. I savor

her mastery of the *pivot*,
a word embodying two meanings,
furu read as *falling* and *aging* simultaneously
as flower and body blend in her poem.

Tonight, I am my own pivot—
this Japanese assent to the body of sorrow,
and this Roman ferocity
as I stare at my mother—
her arthritic fingers opening
as winter flowers in angry bloom.

One Life Worth Living

Gary is painting the bathroom today,
clean & sober after destroying
his big Hollywood gig painting the homes of stars,
now cleaning his brushes in my backyard
happy, after almost dying, to be so
alive. Which starts me writing
as the solar orb we both bask in
steals into my poem like an orange Samurai
slashing the air with Haiku, which my son texts me,
just now, from Boston in snow: tiny poems
from college on my Apple phone screen—
and though these words are nothing
but cartoon dialogue balloons appearing
white then blue, they are just as miraculous
as Emily's carefully folded poem heresies
secreted under her floor boards, or Walt's
rambling lines that made a poem haul
the entire wild weight of a country
on its black rails. Someone

must make the tiny letters work,
fashion a kind of incarnation in Word
where Gary cleans his brushes,
Walt savors his sprig of wheat,
Emily sits at her wooden table,
knowing the world depends on this
to go on. How the furnace of sun
burns its way into my thumbs
typing miniature Haiku replies
to a boy staring at Boston snow
from his dorm room bed like Basho.

Winter Sun

Sara, our cat, rolls on her back in the driveway
basking in sun, gravel rubbing her silky coat.
This, despite having just escaped once again
the half-blind dog my mother has brought
to live with us. Zen master cat,
escaping fools by perching
on the roof, descending to
the backyard when safe,
one moment
scared out of her mammalian mind,
the next
demonstrating her enlightenment
by cavorting near canine danger on the warm asphalt.
I could be dead, her look suggests,
but forgives me the brooding carnivore brought to our house
because Jack Gilbert says,
There is laughter every day in the terrible streets of Calcutta,
so we should do no less. Which is difficult
to take from a cat since I'm supposed
to be one-up on the chakra chain
from this feline provocateur. Still,
she has a point: though there is never
an end to the wanton dangers
of this mischievous life—
my mother's stroke,
her blind dog's zealotry,
my own death lurking
unceremoniously ahead—
there is this light
in the driveway's gravel,
my cat and I,
soft bellies exposed,
a purr in the throat.

Four Stitches, a Few Bucks

My eighty-three year old mother
blinks past the blood snaking down her cheek
from the purpled gash on her forehead,
says, *I'll bet you're going to put this in a poem.*

Of course, I'd no immediate thought
of this, despite my reputation.
Had hoped to be writing this morning—
but a good son takes his mother to the doctor
after she's finally moved in to our house,
reaches up to the top shelf in the closet
of her new room, grabs a White Zinfandel
from its cardboard container to celebrate,
miscalculates as a second bottle slips and falls,
whacks her on the forehead, somehow
not knocking her out. She'd bravely
bandaged the wound and gone to sleep
till I noticed this morning and whisked her off
to Urgent Care instead of writing a poem.
Though, of course, the wait is now over an hour,
so we dab the blood with a tissue,
decide the bandage can manage fine till then,
take her modest retirement check
and open a bank account in this her new town.

It is an awkward circle from cradle to urn,
but my mother traverses this arc with grace.
Sometimes you just roll with the punches,
make the minutes count, make them pay:
a few bucks, a few stitches, a glass
of pink sparkling wine, a little poem,
and you can go on.

The Congregation of the Blank Page

My Dad is writing poems through me,
though I'd never admit as much in court.
But in a poem, you can get away
with most anything, even the claim
that a father, who in life was a preacher,
might indeed haunt his son in a tender way,
stand behind the poem's pulpit, keep talking.
Knowing the veil between eternity and mortality,
while opaque, is not soundproof.

Nor is this his first experience with poetic mediumship,
having left his pastorate not only to teach
Junior High, but to trance-channel
twelve spirits—New Age ruminations,
nothing Armageddon—my mother
typing what my father spoke, pages
piling up in big black binders on the shelf
till his death.

But why stop there, I imagine my father saying.
Once you've got the hang of it,
why ever in this world would you stop?

So when I sense that particular rustle
in the ethers, I lend him my tongue,
the bones in my fingers, let him say
the everything he couldn't in just one life—
feel him peer out over the congregation
of the blank page, speak.

Valentine's Day

Gabriel, my son, *busks* poems in a Boston subway terminal,
minting handfuls of black typewriter words on bookmarks
for spending money at college, while the snow
pounds the city with its delicate white fists.

My daughter Kelsey teaches history to ninth-graders
here in Santa Cruz, texts me a photo of her
extra-credit question about who the best football team
in the world is (of course, San Francisco
being the only answer worth coin),
and another about who the German mystic
Hildegard of Bingen was. I reply
that her soaring chants in
A Feather on the Breath of God ring
from my iPod playlist each morning,
eliciting a "No joke!"
as Kelsey piles in a car with friends
bound for Tahoe's snowy mountains.

And just about the time my children
leave me stranded in an empty house
with a heart rubbery as a rodeo clown
running from the horned bull aiming to spear me,
Mother moves in with Father's memories
brimming in her eyes, and how can I resist
these days—evaporating like snow
on my cheeks in the old hot tub
with my wife on Valentine's,
the moon full of light,
eyes full of rain.

The Minotaur's Lair

My wife calls from an icy road outside the Kentucky hospital,
having escaped for a moment her mother's obsession
with the million dollars waiting for her in Jamaica,
her entire wracked and hollowed body lunging
toward the door, commanding her daughter
to undo the lock—but there is no secret code
for the mind's labyrinthine maze. And so
my wife follows the thin thread she's laid
in her heart from the bullish Minotaur's lair
where the death of every parent snorts
its angry inevitability—runs
from that blind grief back
towards her husband
along the strands
of cell phone
ethers
as I cup
the small black box
to my ear half a continent away.
Listen
to an alphabet neither
of us can bear—my own mother
after two strokes, shaking her head
as the words disappear, caressing
her blind dog who growls at everything
she can't quite see. And the meaning of growing old
is lost in the brain's bark as it digs for the buried bone
precious beyond measure, lying in the folded gray
of cerebellum. The bone of consciousness—
the million dollar coin—is not in Jamaica. It is beneath
the hoof of the Minotaur stamping the dirt
in the center of grief's maze.

A Beat Prayer in Paris

My son and I sit over cappuccinos
at a wooden table, stir with tiny spoons
the chocolate powder & whipped cream
in Japanese cups—

blue scenes of a kimonoed-woman
and child conversing on a bench,
a samurai leading a saddled horse
away from Mount Fuji.

He'd ambled back from the antiquarian
first edition bookstore at *Shakespeare & Company*
across from Notre Dame

with a Cheshire-cat grin. In hand,
the original British edition of Allen Ginsberg's
Wichita Vortex Sutra, laced with anti-war rants,
vicious indictments of the world's madness.

He paid thirty pounds for the slim volume
held reverently between his pale fingers.
Randomly, I open the brittle pages
to a prayer I might have intoned at his birth:

Communion of bum magicians,
congress of failures from Kansas & Missouri
working with the wrong equations…
O long-haired magician come home
and take care of your kid.

After the separation, its madnesses,
we now sip the bitter brown from cups
flekked with dark sweetness,

the samurai tethering his horse again
at home, the woman and child
blue in their kimonos.

Invoking the Duende

> *Perhaps I can lash its eyes open for you.*
> —Lorca, in New York

Linda leans over the large white cup of hot dark chocolate
at the Octagon café, and loves me. Despite
everything. Her eyes are her name
in Spanish, *beautiful*,

as I recount the wild nameless
that went wrong, a dark bull
horned and lethal raging in

a husband's skull. I tell her
of the poet Lorca's talk
in Buenos Aires in 1933,
how in bullfighting
two *toreros* may fight *al alimon*,
holding one cape between them
to outwit the bull together.

I take her hand, grab
the red fabric of our loving,
with a deft turn together
send the snorting bull,
exhausted, past us
into dust.

The Dionysian Well

At Alberto's Uruguayan Steakhouse in Amsterdam,
we order beer and grilled chicken
sitting outside with our grown kids
in a narrow cobblestone alley
filled with tourists, mainly young,
some gray-haired, curious. Our
conversation drifts to what we,
the parents, did or didn't do when young.
They've figured it out already.
We were children of the 60's & 70's
so how else could it have been?
All they want is a little confirmation.
The four of us stare at each other—
there is no lying, here, a continent away,
our kids almost legal, and hell,
we're all legal in Amsterdam
for almost anything. Marijuana cafes
like Starbucks on every corner,
the red light district with its curved windows,
the prostitutes disdainful till approached,
then all smiles. Not everything
that can be done should be done,
but my wife and I pause, smirk a bit,
then let loose with story after story
that finally has our cocky children, well,
in a bit of awe. Not, I think, at our modest
profligacy, but that the Dionysian well
is dug so deep by each generation.

After dinner, our kids cajole,
send their veteran parents into Amsterdam's night,
tell us to buck-up, stay out late,
invoke some of that old magic. We walk
with unanticipated trepidation, holding hands
like teenagers into the warm night,
passing one intimidating café after another,
wondering if we should call our kids

for more pointers—till the red sign
along a quiet block announces *Rookies*,
and we amble with feigned bravado
straight up to the bar, stare into the Dionysian eyes
of the young man at the cash register as we order,
drift into the mercurial pools
of the old gods.

Anima

In the dream,
she reached for my hand
as if to dance—lost as I was
in some Arab town, perhaps
Northern Africa. Her dress
a faded flower print
of pink and red and peach
which she filled with ample breasts
and hips—beautiful
in that plain way when women
know who they are.

I'd rumbled into town
in an aging Volkswagen van,
confused by foreign streets,
directions shouted in tongues,
gestures pointing all ways at once.
She found me praying in front
of an immense Mosque waiting
for God, or perhaps death, staring
at the dark grandeur of its burgundy
spires turning black in the setting sun.

Grasping my hand, she took me
from this sad obsession
to a villa smelling of lemons and roses
where we ate lamb, dates, yogurt,
sang *jacaras* about pranksters
and vulgar adventures, then
danced to lute & oud with her
tribe of *romani* friends. Laughing,
she said, *I am you—let us be friends*

as we twirled round the room
like dervishes, her eyes asking
Are you lost now?

Enlightenments

The soul is a newly skinned hide...
Only then...

—Rumi

Enlightenment in a Silly Hat

After meditating for hours,
a squat fire-plug of a man appears
in the center of my mind: Otto von Bismarck,
the premier of Prussia in 1862—
storming onto the stage in thigh-high leather boots
and spiked helmet to dominate,
if not Europe, at least my attention.
Otto, it seems, is my ego—
morphed from an odd fragment of morning reading,
insistent on complaining about the world's
failure to give in to his demands.
Hypnotized by such petulant charisma,
I ignore the Zen command to return
to my breath, and indulge fiery Otto
instead. His complaints

do sound like my ego,
a formidable intellect so often deployed
in joyless cunning. His love of food.
And power. Otto is most at home
in a shifting world of intrigue and drama
which he attempts to control.

Yet despite his talk of *dying for the cause,*
which neither my ego nor Otto truly wants to do,
he fears there is no personal triumph in the end,
only his silly helmet; boots with a hole in the sole.

I finally adjust my old legs out of half-lotus,
take a deep breath, put my arm around Otto.
Tell him to sit here quietly, that I've been waiting
to meet him face to face for a long time. That
how you die is as important as how
you live. And with that,

he curls up in my lap and again becomes me—
as the Zen master opens his curious eye
wondering, perhaps, how I manage to sit
and meditate in thigh-high boots
with such a silly,
pointy hat.

Driving Kwan Yin to See Captain America

I spotted her sitting in repose at a statuary
& garden store on the way to Half Moon Bay,
one foot touching the ground,
the other folded elegantly under her body
as she gazed intently at something
either very close, or far beyond my
perception. In a very un-Buddhist way,
I had to have her—the spiritual-materialism
Trungpa warned of. Still, we love our gods,
bought her on the spot while a man named Juan
carried her by wheelbarrow to the passenger side
of my car. Even with Juan's muscled arms and
farm-worker back we struggled to situate
her in the front seat, the carved stone of
her body heavy as, well, ancient stone.
Finally, on old carpet remnants of red
and gray, we perched her so she could
watch the immense Eucalyptus trees
and the sea as we drove home. But
pulling into the driveway alone,
there was no one to help carry her
into the garden. She was in no hurry—
but I was (one of the differences
between us) since I was soon
to be on my way again to see
Captain America in 3-D at the movies.
So, feeling as though I was driving
with a blow-up doll or mannequin
like rebels gaming the car-pool lane,
I nonchalantly parked her downtown
to spend the evening by herself.
Which, I gather, she is used to, though
I imagined her smiling at perplexed passersby
peering in through the car window.
As I entered the theater I swear she was still
with me, whispering in my ear

not to take too seriously this business
of saving the world like a star-spangled superhero.
Better to sit still as stone—people will be just
as curious, just as saved.

Chance Encounter

In San Francisco, I start chatting
with a short-haired woman
sitting next to me at the Pork Store Café
on Haight Street, bright red-frame glasses
girding her Brooklyn born face as she
works her jaw like a bulldog, craning
her short neck toward the *Tricycle*
meditation journal open
on my round table by the window.
Love that magazine, she barks,
explaining she lives just around the corner
when not traveling to Burma,
backpacking each year
through remote villages,
wowing the locals with her
grasp of the language,
the spirit of old stone
temples and stupas.
I tell her my wife
keeps a small flat in the city
down the block from the Zen Center
where she meditates sometimes
after work. My friend smiles,
says one of her best buddies
is an old dog who lives there.
I reply *must be one of the more
enlightened souls,*
and we chuckle together
remembering the Zen koan
about whether a dog has
Buddha nature or not—
of course, the right answer
a booby-prize of sorts,
laughter the only thing
seducing a wink out of
the master. Finally,

it is time to go as she
pauses, says *You know,*
kindness is really my religion,
offers me her hand and says
by the way, my name is Jane,
as in Tarzan. I laugh again
at the coming alliteration, say
my name is Dane, as in the
big dog. Barking our names
out loud over the din
of the café, we cackle
at the absurdity, bow,
usher each other again
into a city every bit as enlightened
as a junk yard dog
howling at daylight
moon.

The Metaphysics of Parking in San Francisco

Angling my white Prius
into a tiny edge of curb
on a short alley street
in the Hayes district,
I give up just as a jaunty
Japanese man in black glasses
and khakis waves me back,
says it's a grand parking spot,
just right for me, don't leave!
He looks mysteriously like
the enigmatic Key-maker
in the Matrix movie, opening
doors that take you halfway
round the world, and suddenly
my dead father is here speaking
through the man's broken English,
gesticulating fiercely as he says
*stay, don't go, there is room enough
here for you!* My father,
who loved all things Japanese
after being stationed there
in the Navy, lingers in family lore
as the wizard of parking spots,
always able to find you one
from the *other side* if you
only pay attention. Believing
this encounter to be one of those
moments, I inch backwards
and forwards repeatedly while
the Key-maker runs from front
to back of my car yelling out
more room, yes, no, stop!
till sure enough I am perfectly
nestled into the smallest
parking spot I've ever seen.
We both laugh out loud

as though some immense
good fortune has just come
to both of us. The ritual,
improbably, repeats several
hours later after returning
from the Arlequin Café
as I sit again in my car trying
to imagine now how to get
out from this tight spot—
and who should show up again
but my father as the Japanese Key-maker
surprised as I at this replay,
his arms waving towards the heavens
as he says *I can't believe it,*
I can't believe it, you again!
He spots me inch by inch
till I emerge once more
free on the small alley,
and we stare at each other
unbelieving. That the unexpected
happens, that even strangers in a city
can matter to each other,
that the dead can return
even if for a moment
to get you in, then out
of the impossible.

Pink Roses

The stone body of the young Buddha statue
sits serenely beneath the pink rose bush
in my backyard, smooth face inured
to the scent of petals profligate
round him. I remember

as a freshman in high school sitting
with an open Bible on my lap in the fragrant grass
while Ted, a rebel Jesus Freak a few years older
stared hard at me after prayer group,
said, *You're too young to lose yourself
like this.* Told me to close the Good Book,
find a girl, take her under the bleachers
at the next football game, smell her perfume,
nibble her ear. I had no idea what he was talking about,
though I suspected he understood something
of desire's impossible nature,
had seen him slip his drummer's hand
under his girlfriend's sweater at the Jesus rock concert,
watched her smile, accept his hand
as though it were God's.

Ted was wiser than the young stone monk
sitting in my backyard unaffected
by the psychedelic pink flowering
before his closed eyes. After all,
even the young Buddha had to become
drunk with desire before it left him empty enough
to escape the prison of the pleasure palace.

Only then did his Third Eye open,
his blood swoon drunk again
at the scent of blossoms
pink, everywhere.

Paradise

is still just around the corner, where it
always seems to lie. As a young boy,

it was a plan of escape, the Rapture
promising to elevate us from failed bodies
at the sound of a trumpet purer than Miles Davis'
pensive horn on my father's stereo.
Or Mother Mary's demure breast
obliquely promising what my mother
and the high school cheerleaders
kept hidden. No one had told me, yet,
how improbable the quest for paradise
is—bankrupt as a heroin dealer's promise,
or a used car dealer's lemon.

Even before Genesis was first scratched
on papyrus, the Babylonians believed
that Enkidu, a wild man living happily with gazelles,
was enticed from Paradise by a woman
wise enough to love by a murky waterhole,
birth civilization. He woke,

as do we all, dazed by the womb—
no longer living inside of Paradise
but armed with nostalgia,
a rebel's recklessness, an iron foot
on the gas pedal of the red Mustang of the body,
reeling toward the horizon's mirage,
yet haunted by the rear view mirror.

Until the wild man wakes one morning
in the ramshackle motel of his life listening
to Miles rather than Jesus, hears his woman
snoring softly beside him cloaked
in twisted bed sheets,

and like Enkidu, begins to understand
that Paradise lies neither forward nor behind,
but in the clunky lemon parked outside,
the enigmatic horn of scratched vinyl,
the gazelle of your heart leaping.

The Grail Molecule

They knew, roughly, what they were looking for
in the frog embryos: the molecule
that instructs each cell
what to do, what to become, where to go.
And finally, there it lay
in a small part of mesoderm underneath
the lip of the blastopore, which
in English, means
they found the gleaming gate of God
guarded by a kind of archangel
past which the encrypted cells
ushered—naïve, unformed,
unlimited—till blessed
to become one thing
and not another.

One biologist said, *We are standing
and walking with parts of our body
that could have been used for thinking…*
stunned at the amorphous genius
lingering nascent in each cell
waiting for this signal
of what to become: if strong,
a spinal cord down the length
of the back; if faint, then
the skin that covers a body.
Other messages encoded
in adjacent tiers of each cell—
a fierce alert becoming muscle,
a steady pulse the kidney,
a whisper: connective tissue
and blood. The body

is genius, empty grail
waiting, like us,
to become what we will,

a jewel held at last
in the fist of the knight
who, all along, believed.

The Noise in My Brain

Mind is a monkey, the Hindus say—
neural fibers hung lobe to lobe
like rainforest vines swung from
by noisy little Macaque-thoughts
in the canopy of gray-matter,
branches descending into the
body's trunk where finally,
beneath the ground, the root
disappears untouched by light.

You can hear them laughing,
just close your eyes, try
to sit still as the monsoon
of the body's multi-phonic
cacophony storms through
chasing even the jaguar
under cover. Only

the fungi of one's darkest
pre-human sensibilities
can speak then, a language
even enlightenment can
barely hear. But then,

a real monkey knows
the obvious: noise
doesn't hurt the forest,
nor clouds the sky.

Beloved

> *Solitude is a fierce lover, jealous—jealous.*
> —Cecelia Woloch

Alone in Poland, a small cottage,
a well to draw water from,
a bucket to pour it into a glass
for the wooden table we dine at

one glass, for the two of us.

Then in Paris, the solitude of cafés,
sitting for hours, roaming
from one coffee to another,
never unfaithful.

One cup, always.

Wandering the avenues,
the waterfront, hand in hand
with myself past a solitary river-boat,
a pigeon, a rusted bicycle
with one torn, empty seat.

But at night, ah, to be with friends,
lay out blackberries, gouda,
sourdough, wine, to laugh.

My beloved is not jealous then—watches
me dance the tango, the flamenco
with anyone; but later, alone in bed,
kisses me firmly on the mouth
like a wild stranger.

In the morning, another kiss—
this time with a poem on the tongue.

The Dreams I Can't Remember

Waking from another long night,
my wife asks, *do you remember your dreams?*

Often, I don't—except for opaque glimpses
into dramas so titan even Napoleon would be pleased.
The ones you wake from in a cold sweat,
or swathed in erotic glow. Just enough
to confirm what scientists say,
that we dream like drunks, oblivious
the morning after.

It is the amnesia that intrigues me. Not
just my own, but theirs: these fugitive
dream selves who ignore this waking one.
Rarely does my doppelganger pause
to ponder me—the names of my children,
the rough asphalt of my street,
the weathered skin of my hands.
He cavorts with any number of personages
from my life:

a boss, dead relatives, movie-stars, even
my wife. But they are his, in that life, not
borrowed from mine. Even the rare lucid
dream, where I wake in its middle with that
little *aha!* then inevitably decide to fly or
look about for someone to have sex with—
even then it is he, the dreamer, who is awake.
Unconscious of my sleeping body

curled round the soft limbs of my wife
who lies slumbering next to me—
a legion of dream wives stirring under her eyelids,
murmuring through her pink lips.

As the Indigo Girls Sing

about looking for meaning by smoothing
the wrinkles from a cloth,
I iron a crumpled shirt for work
as a therapist helping others to press
life's endless ripples smoother.

And there are so many.

I could become obsessive
ironing the stubbornness from clients,
children, wife, my own irreparable self—
each sprayed with fine mist
to smooth away imperfection.
But the Cosmos

also sings to me, astronomers calculating
that the Big Bang expanded the universe
evenly in all directions except for small imperfections
in the cosmic fabric, wrinkles which began to glow
like endless strands of Christmas tree lights
strung across a vast night—early stars
going nova, heavy atoms forged
in their dying cauldrons coalescing
into planets, each mistake becoming
the very matter we are made of. So,

as the Indigo Girls croon, I remember
being human lies in the imperfections
that allow us to be. That make me,
nonetheless, obsessive:

whistling Shakespeare,
muscling my arm against
each blemish, every wound.

Comeback

Jogging along a forest path ruminating on my failures, I come across orange-garbed young prisoners on work detail from the county jail, shovels deep in mud dredging a trench for rain run-off. A hardened crew supervisor walks toward me to make sure there's no trouble, I guess, from his detainees. But I smile, say "Hey!" in greeting, and having broken the ice, a line of faces smile back at me, wary, happy for the diversion. One muscled, Hollywood handsome man notices my black and yellow Lakers shirt, says *Did ya see the game last night?* And I say "No, who won?" *Spurs by one.* I grimace big down the line, say "Fuck!" And this young guy at the end laughs, blurts out *He said fuck!* And suddenly we're weirdly bonded, nine young toughs and one aging white-haired jock, as the sun filters down through redwood and oak, shovels paused, our sweat mingling in the cool air. I say "Yea, I been depressed since the Lakers lost to Boston on their home court, so haven't been watchin'" and they nod. You can almost feel the heartache in the air, broken hope, getting drubbed on your home court, America. But the inmate with the Hollywood-looks offers a wry, irrepressible smile, says *Yea, but we'll be ready come playoff time, that's when it counts.* I look him in the eye, then work my middle-aged legs back into motion up the hill, signal a thumbs-up to the long line of orange and mud and dreams.

Sacrament

Officiating their wedding, I remember
that night years before in the mountains,
the mattress on the floor in the maroon forty-foot trailer,
how we three lay in the heat of the summer evening,
her body between us, talking of music, of kissing.
We were young, when the heart could believe
anything was possible. So he paused,
raised an eyebrow, looked at me, winked at her,
said *you want to see something?* I of course said *yes*
as she pulled her shirt up over her small breasts.
Now put your mouth on her nipple, his lips performing
the same sacrament on the other red areola.
We suckled in awe, her face transfiguring
as a wave arched through her belly,
into her eyes, and she, after, content,
smiled as a god might at her supplicants.
I remember this as I marry them
to each other—have a stake in their music,
still want to believe love is all,
how once I lay innocent and
holy at her breast.

Wild Weeds

We were sweeping his father's driveway,
contemplating whether kissing a guy
would be anything like kissing a girl.
After we'd dated the same woman in college,
he'd offered me a summer job painting houses
so we could philosophize, determine
the true nature of the world. His face
was aquiline, wisp of goatee, full lips.
That afternoon we examined the question
of kissing from every angle while we swept:
how a woman parts her lips, slips her tongue into you.
How men might do this with each other. Pausing
next to his pile of leaves, he cocked
his head, seemed to consider the curve
of my cheek. Our eyes locked. I felt
he might take a step toward me,
but the moment passed, and, smiling,
we grasped the wooden handles again,
began to sweep the lingering questions
of desire back into the lot adjacent —
where wild weeds flowered in scandalous bloom.

Monkey Mind

The Zen teacher rings the bell to meditate,
admonishes: *watch your breath.*
Because the mind is a monkey, insatiable.
But seated on my zafu, I muse
that inventiveness is in our DNA.
Gunpowder, rocketry, wheelbarrows, cast iron,
the compass, paddlewheel boats, block-printing,
stirrups, paper-making, mechanical clocks—
all from Buddhist China despite centuries of meditation.
Busy monkeys indeed. But *watch your breath,* he says,
because in the West it is now the atom,
bombs of hydrogen and neutron,
the nuclear physics of relentless unbounded energy
exploding in our synapses, our bicameral minds
wanting, wanting
and the answer is too often *yes.*
Watch your breath, he intones, because this monkey
is relentless as addiction, sucking form from the void,
blowing it back into the world as the opium-smoke
of the mortal. *Breathe in, breathe out* he says,
the heart its own pulse, sufficient.

I sigh, unfold my legs at the break,
reach for a banana in my backpack,
peel its tough yellow skin, bite
the ripe fruit into my mouth,
feel desire's dilemma sharp as a Zen koan:
the monkey in me breathing deeper
into every curiosity, into
unfathomable hunger.

A Meditator's Confession

My mind wanders—this is the nature of mind
as every Buddhist knows, thoughts like crows
roaming from telephone pole to vacant field
cawing up a storm. Like this thought,
how I've strayed beyond my own
happiness, sniffing like a hapless dog
into neighbor's yards oblivious of fences,
latches, civilization. Finding bones,
burying bones. Digging them up again.
Gnawing them relentless till only shards
remain. Then, a new bone. A new yard.

I remember my first love in college,
the fine bones in her fingers
as they dipped silk into vats of color,
hung the pieces to dry.
When did first love turn to old love?
How does affection dry, become only art?
Like the crow, become a dark slash
of movement against the steady sky?
Like a dog, become only the new bone
hunted? In mid-life, I'm learning to sit

still enough to enjoy the crows rancorous
in the branches outside. Though my heart
is still a puppy shitting all over the newsprint
laid out in the kitchen—too cute to kill
or maroon to the pound. Buddha knew,

sitting still beneath his tree while all hell
broke loose in his brain that there was no hope
for the mind. It is a crow. A dog. A wonder.

Butt Crack at the Poetry Reading

It was an Oscar quality crack,
completely itself, naked, sincere.
The man whom it adorned
was a lover of poetry
whose immense buttocks were worthy
of a heavyweight plumber down on his knees
in the kitchen, listening to the sound
of pipes, lost in their leaky articulation.
His ample torso crammed into the black
plastic folding chair with the empty space
between back and seat framing like a TV screen
his buttocks' red fleshy cleavage.

Lifting my gaze from his hypnotizing masterpiece,
eyes roaming over shoulder muscles thick
as barn beams, broad bald head,
flared red ears fanned like satellite dishes,
I found myself applauding.
The pugnacious suchness of this man,
leaning into the sound of sentences,
his body the perfect tool
to bear literature's weight,
the tonnage of meaning
down to the evening's last
iron word.

Universal Complaint

Why wouldn't one complain, I thought
sitting near the podium in the bookstore
listening to a mystical cosmologist
describe each of us as holographic fragments
containing the Cosmos—the immense
longing that birthed galaxies fueling
this same irrepressible fire burning
in every molecule of my own being.
This

is a problem, I mused, shifting my pointy
tailbone on the hard chair, leaning through
my chocolate and red wine headache to
listen. If I am a fragment, holographic
no less, of the whole wild thing, Who

in their right mind would unleash such
infinite longing inside one small human
body? No wonder I dream bigger than
I could ever be in one short lifetime,
balancing laziness with a compulsion
to achieve more, always more. It is

maddening—that I am legion, contain
multitudes. That I flame

with the very atoms present at the Beginning,
when something infinitely small and dark
stopped complaining, and went *Bang!*

A Great Civilization

In the island forests of Bolivia before
any white man found them, the Arawak
cultivated lianas thick as a human arm,
blade-like leaves dangling six feet long
and smooth-boled Brazil nut trees,
the thick-bodied flowers smelling like warm meat.
Earth mounds rose above waters cultivated as canals
for travel between spacious villages framed
by moats and palisades, along which they'd walk
in long cotton tunics, heavy ornaments dangling
from wrists and necks. But in 1927,

anthropologists found their descendents living
in constant hunger, no clothes,
no cows or llamas,
no musical instruments,
no art—except necklaces of animal teeth—
unable to count beyond three, no religion,
no conception of the universe. They

thought they'd stumbled upon a primitive
humankind living in the rawness of nature
for millennia—unaware that when the first
Europeans arrived centuries before, influenza
and smallpox raced ahead, bringing
the Arawak to their knees. And no one

knew, till now: scientists piecing together
records of teeth, shards of pottery,
eco-analysis and *voila!*
a great mysterious culture heretofore
unknown emerged from the mists
of history. Might we too—

this culture of moon travel,
the great web of internet,
an entire library of world music
in the palm of a hand—one day

be discovered again, as
barefoot entrepreneurs
having lost it all.

Holding On

The black Jaguar's silver license plate frame says
    Insured by Jesus, Smith & Wesson

which seems somehow so American,
this romantic breeding of religion
with guns. And the Jaguar,
after cruising the asphalt jungle with its
effortless arrogance, has found momentary
rest between the white lines of this parking spot.
I don't know if the driver gained by sweat or inheritance
this luxury, lingering somewhere
between prayer and fear that this glimmering
metallic heaven

could be dented or stolen by the rogue Fates,
or perhaps the IRS, or any number of have-not's
roaming still hungry inside this First World
of privilege. But as I stare

at the immaculate Jaguar, older than I'd expected,
I watch a humble receptionist emerge from the
building adjacent, tenderly wipe the dirt
from the silver panther ornament leaping
from the hood. Realize she is simply bent
on protecting this used-car deal of an old
American Dream she probably paid cash for

as it sat on the lot, day after day,
waiting for anyone
who could still afford it.

The Privilege of a Private Life

In Karachi, human life goes on
tipsy balance: scandalously happy,
then uncompromising in sorrow.

Loved for cricket & conversation,
feared by foreigners for chaos.
Living

for spiced tea, a good book
amid religious violence
radical uncertainties,

the *self*
becomes even more ambiguous

than in the confines of peace. The

privilege of a personal life, inviolate,
an American promise. An

Eleventh Commandment:
thou shalt not touch me.

Here, it is heresy—
and broken, broken.

While Listening to Nelson Mandela's Memorial

At the stop light, I idle
behind a cheery yellow Volkswagen Bug,
two University students inside and
at first I think they, too, are singing
to the radio's riotous music,
bouncing in their seats wildly,
hands waving in the air—but then
the passenger's face turns toward the driver
in rage and he is not singing but yelling,
face distorted like a demon. He spits
at the man or woman behind the wheel
who explodes as the car becomes a bizarre
mixed martial arts scene of flying elbows,
fists, saliva. Stunned, I honk loudly,
momentarily interrupt their rave
as the light turns green and the yellow car
speeds ahead. I return to the radio again,

listen to Mandela's memorial in South Africa,
think of his years in that prison cell,
the violence of it all. Still
how he rose, fitted one bruised arm
then another into the sleeves of
his multi-colored shirts, lifted
a country from its dark trance,
each morning, every midnight,
the yellow sun rising,
the moon rising, disappearing—
how small I feel in the face of it
obsessed with my own grievances.
How I want Nelson to rise from the cold
concrete floor of my amygdala,
lay a hand on this reptile brain
like he must have those long years
when instinctual rage, the logical response,
would only kill you more. So
wherever you are, whoever you are

in that little VW Bug—or Texas,
Moscow, Oval office—
let us take the little fist of the soul,
pry open each finger, the thumb,
wave our hands in the air
like the fools we are,
sing.

Your Thousand Faces

Walking down the street, I notice
an older woman looking at me from the opposite curb,
and realize I have no idea what she sees.

Is it her alcoholic son convicted of arson
somehow sobered and poised, or perhaps

a long lost lover, the secret no-one knew. We
are randomly seen in an endless cascade

of public and private moments, and like
the grey-bearded gentleman in the coffee line

two patrons in front who I fiercely love because
he reminds me of my dead father—none of us

know the thousand faces

we wear for others. How a stranger, or unsuspecting
office-mate, or neighbor, someone who sees you

on stage, or cursing a traffic light, distracting
a moth from flame, or blithely ignoring

the stranded motorist you're sure is a serial killer—
how a multitude of disparate moments haunt our identities

unseen. Held in the mercurial perceptions of others.
Maybe this is what we behold, upon death, our

thousand faces unveiled through the eyes of all
we encountered, however fleetingly. This

the sum one can never know in life, except for
the glimpse, here, in the mirror
of another's eyes.

Caedere

I am stunned, each time, at the violence implicit
in choice. Linguists know

the word decide sharing a root
with homicide. The Latin *caedere* means
to cut down or to kill. No wonder

death scents every life
with rose petals, white bones,
dying horoscopes. The horns

of any meaningful dilemma pierce the body
so it is impossible to walk away whole. The
red muscle held captive by ivory ribs only

dreaming of a field where all things come to be.
While the delicate labyrinth of gray matter
takes as hostage the lost lives

it will never live, tucks them into catacombs
prays for resurrection. In the meantime, I live

a hundred daily deaths. Or now,
walking away from you,
just this one.

Marginalia

In olden days, writing in the margins of rare texts
was proof of engaged reading
rather than bad manners
or graffiti.

Your own strange facts, obdurate opinions, illustrations,
just as important as the original text—
recopied from antiquity on parchment rare
and expensive.

One marginalium to Homer's *Iliad*
goes on at great length about earthworms,
comparing their emergence from soil to the soul's emergence
from divine light.

A manuscript of Vitruvius in the Bodleian Library
finishes off the *Ten Books on Architecture* with a recipe
for curing hemorrhoids with white bean paste and oil of violet.

A fifteenth-century copy of Boethius' *Consolation of Philosophy*
has a self-portrait of the manuscript's red-haired owner
moping melancholically as he says *Console me, Mother Philosophy—
an evil woman has done me wrong!*

Many medieval manuscripts enshrine tiny blocks
of ancient text afloat
in a vast sea of personal commentary.

A reader
may find meaning in the margins
more than the great tenets of truth—

a balm for angst

in oil of violet,
in the flaming red hair of the personal.

Diaspora

Wandering in San Francisco for the day,
I stumble upon the Museum of the African Diaspora,
enter double glass doors into a gaggle
of young black students in the foyer.
Puzzled for a moment at my white-bearded presence,
we smile at the first display describing
how all living people belong to the original Diaspora
from East Africa's Rift Valley, each of us
traceable 160,000 years ago to Ethiopia.

Together we enter a corridor of computer-generated
faces and clothing morphing into the vast range
of skin-tone, facial features, adornments
which humans now bear & wear; then
touch-screens playing a range of music—
tribal, gospel, blues, jazz—that never would
have birthed without this cross-pollination
of suffering & art, this blending of French
& Caribbean, Spanish-African-Muslim,
Jewish-downright-fundamental-Christian
inter-continental DNA-scattering
abstract painting of one people into many.

By the time we reach the end on the third floor,
begin our descent down stairs flanked
on one side by a thousand faces colored
coffee & black & brown & white—
I know I have been in exile
from this shared origin. Perhaps
a single tree on a savanna, where
a woman looked at a man
with a secret wish, said
let's lie down for a while,
make a family.

Spiritual Panhandling

A one-legged Tibetan monk on a single crutch
approaches me dressed in worn burgundy & yellow
outside St. Patrick's Cathedral,
places a plastic golden Buddha amulet
in my hand, then a small wrist-band
of wooden prayer beads on my arm,
and smiles. The dark brown beads
are simple, beautiful, and I now
want to believe, really, anything
he has to say. However,
speaking no English,
he can only point to a small black book
which he flips open
like a newspaper reporter
revealing a worn picture
of a Tibetan monastery
scotch-taped inside the cover,
with a list of scrawled names
on the slender white pages
opposite a column for
$20 donation notations.
I do believe his eyes,
fetch the bill from my wallet
and place it in his hand
just like that. Whether
this gesture helps
erect an immense timber
painted golden in some remote
exiled monastery, or, really,
just helps a poor one-legged monk
to eat, or God forbid, enjoy
a pint of Tongba or Raksi,
I will never know. But today,
it is enough to give, see
the laughter in his brown eyes,
the hop in his one good leg.

The Prophet Motive

—from an A.P. Wire Report

The newspaper article from Tel Aviv
touts a school for modern-day soothsayers—
fifty dollars and forty classes later,
the Cain and Abel School for Prophets
will anoint you in T-shirt with cell phone
rather than wooden staff, electronic tablet
rather than stone. The line

between blasphemy and revelation
can be narrow, I know, having wobbled
my way daily across this poetic tightrope.
Is this ecclesiastical hunch, each and every
one of them, filling my body with Allah's
divine smoke, Yahweh's blood, Krishna's
apricot nectar? Or is it merely a dark
Sumatra Expresso Roast coffee barking
through my veins like a coyote-trickster,
cackling at my gullibility—that I,
of all the lost ones, would know anything
worth its cream. Well,

the school advertises nothing about parting
the Red Sea, nor predicting the future
(the old prophets loved this stuff). Rather
it offers classes on the meaning of dreams,
the mysteries of spirit, and how to discern
whether a person's inner knowing is from God
or simply wish fulfillment. *I'm not so sure*

there is a difference, the prophet in me
writes in this poem just now, the garden
outside my window languid with rain,
Peruvian lily, rose petal, lemon branch,
each tart yellow globe a world of divine
wish. And the old withered apple tree

I thought dead, with its tiny green buds
sprouting again, and the future
like the fog rolling in,
so deliciously uncertain.

The Guru

When police broke into his room
at the famous Oregon ashram
after reports of guns, abuse, political threats,
he sighed: *At last, I don't have to pretend to be enlightened.*
Put down the hashish, turned off the video player,
surrendered. Movies and drugs

his constant companion for years
when not lauded as God by his devotees,
waving from one of his many Rolls-Royces
during afternoon drives along the ashram roads,
or moving silky among women
in ecstatic Kundalini dances,
reaching beneath their purple robes
to caress the nipples on their breasts,
raise them to heaven. I had all his books,

was seduced by his message that life was easy
if you let it be. When my Berkeley girlfriend turned up
in a purple robe with the guru's little face
dangling from the wooden beads around her neck,
I surrendered too because I wanted to still sleep with her.
And believe him, about life's mysterious ease.
But it didn't last,

the girlfriend nor the guru. Years later,
grappling with lost bliss, I wondered what went wrong.
He was a good guru, she was a good lover.
At what point, when you're somebody's god,
do you begin poisoning the town well, bring in machine guns,
just beg the police to end it all.

Self-Awareness in the Modern Age

The sperm whale has the largest brain of anyone,
and John Lilly, a scientist, reckoned
it the greatest philosopher on Earth.
Of course, this was the Sixties

when god-whales and divine dolphins
were as common as female activists wishing to make love to them,
dressed in skin-tight leotards, mouths brightly rouged
to help the cetaceans read their lips up close. John
would invite them all in—scientists, women—to study
self-awareness,

stimulate the brains of dolphins, engage
in cortical mapping, see how human they are.
Intelligence

assuming humans as the standard,
which was confusing since U.S. Navy funds
helped build the facility where the military hoped to train
dolphins to carry bombs. Ignoring his funders,
John took LSD suspended in a flotation tank,
injected dolphins with the hallucinogen to see if they too
might become enlightened. Or perhaps
already were, and were humoring us
along the way?

In response, two young males
—Delphi & Pan—
deliberately positioned themselves
in front of a large mirror suspended in water,
watched themselves pretend copulation,
doggy-style. Impeccable dolphin grins

just begging poor John to interpret
this slippery question of intelligence,
and enlightenment, and irony.

The Gift of The Fallen

I remember the fierce brow of the archangel
standing on the dark hill as in Dore's wood-engraved print,
Michael's chin jutted like marble
over we who had fallen so far.

His nose, revolted at the stench of losing.
The massive shoulder bearing thick-limbed wings
that never fail. To never fail. I remember this
conceit, don't you? How he stared at heaven's rebels,
we who dared more

lying broken on unforgiving ground. To never risk
anything. Michael's immaculate foot, muscled
with sure-footed divinity, poised to leap back

to perfection. But it was ruined now, for him.

Heaven would always be the same, unrelenting beauty
staining golden eyes with inescapable light.

Except here, at the bottom of the dark hill.
The swarm of fallen angels already naked, wingless,
digging about in the dirt for what even he could never have
without failure: a life

singular, his own.

This Living

Lucifer was the first to return, just as he'd been the one
to leave at the beginning. The years thick as bats

in the cave of the mad world he'd made. He had done this,
no God banished such a confident child. Walked

to the edge and leapt. Alone. But what they'd done
in his name through the inglorious centuries, all

manner of evils, following him blind
into that infallible black radar of loneliness.

Upside down amid the fallen legion, alone, together.
It takes almost forever to exhaust it.

This inconceivably small singularity of self.
But when it collapses

under the weight of its own isolation, the nova
reaches even to heaven. He was the first

to return. With a new firmament of burnt giants
and brilliant dwarfs wrapped round him like a cloak.

This was all he could do: stumble across the threshold,
feel the hands that bore him from his mother's infinite body

steady him, the unbearable look in her eye as she
stared—loving every eon, each universe, his happy

broken heart.

This Buick of a World

Sometimes I feel like a kid in the back seat of this world,
God at the wheel, whipping his head around
to yell *Don't make me pull over and stop!*
when we carouse too violently.
Mom rolling her eyes as if to say,
Oh don't take him too seriously,
though the patience of even this Madonna
ebbs at our unrelenting entreaties:
Are we there yet? Are we there yet?
Hey that's not fair, he touched my side,
she lied to me, I'm hungry,
are we there yet? Are we there?
As though arrival were the point,
not this rollicking good ride
barreling down the highway
listening to stories about road signs like
Watch for Falling Rock,
son of the great chief Rising Sun.
How we keep scanning the roadside
for this lost warrior, faces glued
to the wide Buick windows
desperate to catch sight of this father's boy
so that we too might be found
when we wander and fall. Then it's back
to bouncing on our butts till the old
coiled wire of the back seats sag,
the silver rear window rollers
with the porcelain knobs at the end
are knocked to the floor,
and God, aging centuries with each
passing minute, sticks a finger in his ear
as though turning down the volume
of the hearing aid he'd just invented
till each prayer becomes a whisper.
We fall asleep dreaming of a world big as a Buick
taking us anywhere we want
in this fallen world,
winged tail lights flaring
red in the dark.

Neighborhood Walk to Circle Market

The red faced young man,
drunk or high on god knows what,
bicycles by singing a little song:
Cruelty is never necessary,
repeating the one line over and over
in a child's sing-song voice. I remember

Mort Marcus' story of the pompous Iowa
Writers' Workshop professor dissecting
a young poet's poem with the precision
of a surgeon and Mafia hit man rolled into one.
How Mort had enough of his bullying,
stood up, told the baffled professor to
"step outside", repeated the threat
when the professor blustered
"oh I think there's a misunderstanding here"
and Mort said "I thought so".

There are different kinds of bravery
and kindness. Who knows
what the drunken bicyclist
had endured to evoke
his binge song. Perhaps
a cruel father, broken beer bottle
or lit cigarette stubbed against skin,
intoxicated lyric the only voice
his ruined heart could muster.
Or the young poet Mort saved from assassination
in a country already bent
on throttling dissent. There
are different kinds of cruelty,
each one personal. I think

of this entering the Circle Market
named for the round street it perches on,
the grocer in halting English
baffled at the neighbor who'd handed him fifty dollars

just to tide him through the latest
robbery. A small kindness
stronger perhaps than any thief's attempt
to steal his immigrant heart.

Walking home with my gallon of milk,
I pass the tiny Missionary Baptist Church on the corner,
the preacher's sermon so loud
the old building shakes. There is
cruelty in how small the black church is
in this white neighborhood,
but beauty too:

like the drunken bicyclist singing,
the poet wagging his fist,
the grocer refusing the neighbor's money ever again,
the preacher shaking the rafters
with thunder.

Special Thanks

Many thanks to the *Emerald Street Writers* critique group, for the camaraderie, good wine, keen eyes, generous hearts and good stories over these many years.

Additional thanks to the varied supporters of poetry and the arts in Santa Cruz, California—including *Poetry Santa Cruz, Santa Cruz Writes, The Tannery* and *Catamaran Literary Reader,* regional literary journals such as *Porter Gulch Review, Red Wheelbarrow, phren-Z, Monterey Poetry Review,* as well as the wide variety of reading series hosted by venues diverse as the University of California, Santa Cruz, to local bagel shops, galleries, and libraries.

My writing would not have been possible without the inspiration of good teachers (whether by workshop or written word), which include Ellen Bass, Gary Young, Robert Sward, Joseph Stroud. For a review of their work and what it represents in the current state of poetry, review my essay entitled *The Manifest Destiny of Language* available online at TriQuarterly. For good measure, read also *The Church of Poetry* available online at CONTRARY magazine; *Why I Love Tony Hoagland: Towards a Post-Modern Humanism* in the Iconoclast.

As ever, love and appreciation to my family and extended community, who both anticipate and recoil from living within the sphere of a poet—as in, *I know that's going into your next poem!* Said with mixed humor and horror...

Endnotes

Kung Fu of the Dark Father (page 13): David Carradine starred in the 1970's television series *Kung Fu,* about a wandering Shaolin monk who travels the American Old West armed only with his spiritual training and skill in martial arts.

Moonbeam at the Destruction Derby (page 19): The actual name of this childhood icon, and avenue, is *Moomjean,* though folks would often hear, and say, *Moonbeam*—hence the poem's title.

The Achilles Stone (page 20): While there is no such mythic stone per se, the thrown stone in the poem is equivalent to the vulnerability of the warrior Achilles' ankle, or in this case the heart of the young child.

The *Glossolalia* of Poetry (page 24): The term references the phenomenon of "speaking in tongues", whereby worshippers are overcome by the Holy Spirit and speak in random syllables akin, say, to jazz "scatting" where sound is more the medium than meaning per se.

A Simpler Rapture (page 29): The "Rapture" refers to the anticipated "second coming of Christ" when true believers will be taken into heaven, leaving the rest of us to fend for ourselves in this lost world. Though kissing is its own reward.

Clay Feet (page 45): Extra points to the reader if you can guess the names of the various gurus represented.

Complex (page 48): Yes, this is a true Freud story. As are all the poems about historical figures in this volume, in one way or another.

Icarus in a Canoe (page 49): Meriwether Lewis was afflicted, and blessed, with a Bi-polar condition before the diagnosis had a name. Which, like Icarus, helped him on his extraordinary journey—yet brought both finally to ground.

Rock'em Sock'em Robots (page 62): In psychoanalytic theory, a child's identification with the same-sex parent is the successful resolution of the Oedipus complex—where every son strives to overcome, then identify with his father in all his ambiguity and complexity.

The Minotaur's Lair (page 79): In Greek mythology, the Minotaur was a creature with the head of a bull and the body of a man, who dwelt at the center of the Labyrinth. Theseus used a ball of thread given him by Ariadne to retrace his steps after confronting the Minotaur in the Labyrinth.

Anima (page 84): In Jungian Analytical Psychology, the Unconscious in a man manifests as the feminine archetype *Anima*; in a woman, the masculine archetype is the *Animus*. Carl Jung states "The encounter with the Shadow is the 'apprentice-piece' in the individual's development…the Anima/Animus is the 'masterpiece'." Jung viewed this encounter as one of the sources of creative ability. It is said the key to working with one's Anima/Animus is to recognize it when it manifests, and exercise our ability to discern the inner Anima/Animus from external reality.

Driving Kwan Yin to See Captain America (page 89): Kwan Yin is the bodhisattva of compassion in Buddhism.

A Great Civilization (page 111): Readers are referred to Charles C. Mann's carefully documented book, *1491 — New Revelations of the Americas Before Columbus*

The Guru (page 124): More extra points to the reader if you can identify this guru.

About the Author

Dane Cervine's books include *How Therapists Dance* (2013) and *The Jeweled Net of Indra* (2007) from Plain View Press. Early collections include his own publication of the book *What a Father Dreams* (2005), as well as a chapbook series under the One Pony Press imprint. His poems have been chosen by Adrienne Rich for a National Writers Union Award; by Tony Hoagland as a finalist for the Wabash Poetry Prize; a Second Place prize for the Caesura Poetry contest; twice a finalist for, and the 2013 winner of the Atlanta Review's International Poetry Prize; 2nd Prize in the 2013 Morton Marcus Poetry Award; and nominated for a Pushcart Prize. Dane's work has appeared in a wide variety of journals including The Hudson Review, The SUN Magazine, Atlanta Review, Sycamore Review, Poetry Flash, Catamaran Literary Reader, Red Wheelbarrow, numerous anthologies, newspapers, video & animation—including a fine press broadside of his poem *Clay Feet* from Sam Amico's Middle Earth press.

Dane lives in Santa Cruz, California—where he works as a therapist, and is the emeritus Chief of Children's Mental Health for the county. His work integrates the arts of therapy and writing with a long-standing meditation practice.

Visit his website at www.DaneCervine.typepad.com.

www.ingramcontent.com/pod-product-compliance
Lightning Source LLC
Chambersburg PA
CBHW052055070526
44584CB00017B/2196